YOGA, PTSD AND ME

A little book to help you help yourself.

Sara Waymont

Sway Arts

Sara Waymont
Sway Arts
wwwyogaptsdandme.com

Disclaimer
To reduce and avoid injury, always check with your doctor, mental health professional or other medical professional before beginning any exercise programme.
If you are unsure about performing any of the techniques described in this book, please seek the advice of a reputable and knowledgeable Yoga Teacher, who will be able to offer further guidance and assistance in a 'live' environment.
Sara Waymont is not and will not be responsible or liable for any injury or harm you sustain as a result of performing any of the postures, Yoga Nidra exercises, breathing exercises or meditation techniques described in this book.
All postures, exercises and techniques described herein are performed entirely at the reader's own risk.
The information provided is not intended to replace medical advice offered by a physician or other licensed health care provider, including mental health professionals and you should always seek the help or advice of a medical professional/ mental health professional if you feel in any way frightened, anxious or unsafe after engaging in yogic practices. You should consult your health care provider before commencing any of the yogic practices described herein.
All postures, exercises and techniques described within this book are suggested as an adjunct therapy and not a replacement for traditional therapy or any other therapy or medical treatment that you are already receiving.

Yoga, PTSD and me/ Sara Waymont. -- 1st ed.
ISBN 978-1-7173674-0-2

This book is dedicated to all of my teachers, past, present and future for feeding the ravenous curiousity within me.

'Rise by that which makes you fall.'

— SWAMI JANAKANANDA

CONTENTS

CHAPTER ONE

INTRODUCTION

I know trauma because I've lived it in a prolonged and visceral way for over a decade.

That's what makes this book different from the many others that discuss trauma and its effects. I'm not an academic writing about trauma. I'm a survivor who's been through the darkness and made her way back out into the light.

And it was yoga that showed me the way.

Yoga doesn't take away life's struggles. It just teaches us to face them with equanimity; a real sense of calmness and composure.

My aim in writing this book is to share with you everything that I've learned so far. I invite you to experiment with the practices and techniques that I've found helpful and to see if they will work for you as well.

At the end of the book there's a list of 'Stuff That I've Learned' (STILs) during my time living with trauma. These are guiding principles that help me to live my life in the safest and happiest way possible. My priority with these is always to protect myself, so that I can be more loving and supportive to others, without compromising my own mental and emotional stability.

Protecting and prioritising yourself isn't a selfish endeavour. It's only once you find peace within yourself that you become the kind of person who can truly live at peace with others.

You can choose to adopt my STILs if you like or you can come up with some of your own. There's a space for that at the end of the text if you want to try it.

There are also 'Things To Remember' (TTRs) scattered throughout the chapters. These are little hints and tips, maybe about practice or perhaps elaborating on a point made in the main text.

Finally, I've included a number of different exercises, as well as information on the Yin *asanas* (yoga forms), which you might like to try as you read through.

And so, before we begin, I'd just like to offer you this pearl of ancient wisdom:

TTR: Struggle in this life is inescapable and inevitable, but suffering is optional.

Things are as they are.

We only suffer because we imagine different.

CHAPTER TWO

LOVING-KINDNESS

I'm not a clinician.

I'm not a therapist or a medical professional of any kind.

I'm not even an especially experienced yoga teacher.

What I am is uniquely qualified in the lived experience of interpersonal trauma.

I say 'uniquely', not because I'm the only person ever to have experienced it, but because everyone's experience with trauma is different. Everyone's reaction to trauma varies and is determined to a large extent by their own level of resiliency (more on this subject later) prior to the event.

I'm the only person who can tell you about how my trauma affected me, in the same way that you are the only person who can tell others about how your trauma has affected you.

I'm also the only one who can tell you about the combination of alternative therapies that I've successfully used to overcome my trauma and how I've used these practices to help others.

> *TTR: There are plenty of things that will help your healing journey.*
>
> *I strongly advise keeping a self-reflective journal that you complete, if not every day, then whenever you feel upset or triggered or especially happy.*
>
> *Art can be a useful pursuit, as well as creative writing, outdoor activities, exercise in general and music.*
>
> *Find an activity (or combination of activities) that work for you.*
>
> *This book isn't the end of your self-healing path. It's just here to show you how you might take those first few crucial steps.*

These days I work as a Complementary Therapist. I use therapeutic art, yoga and the principles of TRiM/ trauma theory to empower other people to help themselves regain their sense of agency.

I work with a whole range of different people; people diagnosed with dementia (a very unique kind of trauma), women who've had miscarriages, people suffering from anxiety, those going through divorce and military veterans to name just a few.

I'm really not picky about who I work with, just as trauma isn't selective in who it hurts.

There are many, many different kinds of trauma and pretty much everyone will experience a traumatic event in one form or another at some point in their lives. Whether it's the end of a relationship, the loss of a loved one, losing your job or something else entirely, this may still feel traumatic to you.

Different events have different significance to each individual.

We shouldn't judge traumatised people by the scope of their traumatic event, but by the effect that this event has had upon them as a person.

There's no 'one size fits all' formula.

However, there are some common features that every traumatic event (including the accumulation of chronic stress) shares, so, before we really focus on the yoga element of this book, we're going to take a brief look at the biological processes that occur within a traumatised individual.

These processes are the same for everyone who experiences an extremely stressful or traumatic event, so neither you, nor I, are unique in our physiological responses. Any symptoms that you are experiencing are not 'weird' and they certainly don't mean that you're 'crazy'.

Part of the healing process is recognising that you aren't to blame for your body's reactions to your experience. When we realise this, it becomes possible to be just a little bit kinder to ourselves.

Below is a quick exercise I invite you to try, perhaps now or maybe at a later date when you feel more ready. It's based on the Buddhist tradition's Loving-Kindness meditation (*metta bhavana*).

Loving-kindness is about cultivating unconditional and inclusive love, whether one 'deserves' it or not. The word 'love' here may easily be exchanged with 'acceptance', as it really means the same thing.

You may not feel that you or your body deserve love right now and that's OK. Practising Loving-Kindness helps us to break these barriers down, softening our attitude to both ourselves and those around us. Practising Loving-Kindness can help us to take the first steps on our path to healing:

Exercise

1. If you like, begin in a seated (or other) position that is comfortable for you.

2. You might want to give yourself a few moments during which time you allow the body to settle, before bringing your attention to your hands.

3. If it feels comfortable for you, bring the palms together in a prayer position or any other position that you prefer. I invite you to notice any sensations that are present in the fingers and the palms and the backs of the hands.

4. As you breathe in and out, noticing any sensations (or lack of sensations if there aren't any) I invite you to choose a positive statement of affirmation to say aloud or think to yourself.

You could use one of these if you don't yet have any of your own:

- May I be free from inner and outer harm and danger.

- May I be safe and protected.

- May I be happy.

- May I be joyful and at ease.

To begin with, this may well be a big enough step for you to take, and you can simply end the meditation here, after repeating your positive affirmation to yourself a few times.

Later in the book, I have included the full practice for you to try, if you would like to.

By softening our attitude towards ourselves, we are able to soften our attitude towards the world around us. It's far easier to meet the challenges that we face with acceptance rather than resistance. This doesn't mean that you never stand up for yourself, but it does make you more able to choose your battles wisely.

A war waged against yourself is one that you will never win.

This lesson took me a long time to learn, but I got there eventually.

TTR: Treat yourself as you would treat a loved one who was suffering. Be gentle and be kind. Meet yourself with understanding and patience on a daily basis.

CHAPTER THREE

THE STRESS RESPONSE

Stress

Stress is a very general and often over-used term. The term 'stress' in this book, always refers to the damaging kind of stress rather than the helpful kind, which is known as 'eustress'.

We may be stressed in many different ways in this modern world and this stress ranges from the minor to the catastrophic; from standing in line, to missing a work deadline, to witnessing a car accident, to serving in active combat or surviving a natural disaster.

Whatever the stressor, your body's reaction to the stress is exactly the same. It doesn't matter whether a tiger is about to eat you or someone just cut you up; your body will initially react to the stress in exactly the same way. It's only the midline structures of the brain that determine the differences between the two stressors. You can flip the bird at the bad driver and you should probably run away from the big cat (I'm no tiger expert though, so you might want to check on that).

In either case, this is the response that's initiated:

FIGHT – FLIGHT – FREEZE - FLOP

When the mind becomes stressed, the body becomes stressed and a range of physiological changes occur, which prepare the body to fight, flee, freeze or flop (a form of freeze response) in the face of a perceived threat. We might also add 'appease/ tend/ befriend' to our list of reactions, depending upon your personality type and the scenario you face.

In any of the stress reactions, the sympathetic nervous system is activated and a cascade of hormones (adrenaline, norepinephrine, cortisol and endorphins) is released to better enable the body to survive the stressful event:

- Adrenaline prepares us to fight or flee.

- Norepinephrine heightens responsiveness).

- Cortisol conserves energy by curtailing non-essential functions/ functions that would interfere with the fight-flight-freeze-flop response.

- Endorphins reduce panic in order to increase chances of survival and reduce pain in the event of injury or death.

Stress is a natural response to a perceived threat.

However, it doesn't matter whether that threat is minor (e.g. your phone running out of battery) or life-threatening (e.g. a physical assault) your body reacts in the same way to both events.

In fact, more often than not, rather than face a real danger, these days we think ourselves into a state of stress.

"What if I miss that deadline?"

Or

"The trains are running late, I'm going to be late for work!"

In the grand scheme of things, neither of these two things is really worth worrying about and, if you think about it, your worrying won't change the course of events in any case. You can't make a train arrive on time through the power of worry - you can only stress yourself out about its delayed arrival.

These everyday problems are the reason why so many of us in the modern world are chronically stressed. Every time we face a minor stressor our body reacts to it and there may be hundreds of minor stressors in any given day.

This leads to an accumulation of hormones that are not discharged, because we aren't able to use the fight-flight-freeze-flop response in the way that nature intended (i.e. we wouldn't normally physically attack our boss no matter how ridiculous his or her demands). This leads to us living with chronic stress and tension that manifests in various different ways.

You might want to look at the list below and see if you are familiar with any of the tell-tale signs of chronic stress:

- *Anxiety*

- *Insomnia*

- *Depression*

- *Over-eating*

- *Under-eating*

- *Confusion*

- *Being easily distracted*

- *Feeling angry/being quick to anger*

- *Tension; both physical and mental*

- *Low self-esteem*

- *Weight gain*

- Weight loss

- Fatigue

- High blood pressure

- Sleeping too much or too little

- Dissociation

- Self-medication with alcohol and/or drugs

This is by no means an exhaustive list. It merely serves as an example to demonstrate that the undischarged Stress Response can pervade many layers of our physical and mental being. We even grow so accustomed to some of these symptoms being part of our day-to-day state that we stop realising that they are even present.

The following exercise gives you a chance to assess your own state:

Exercise:

If you want to, on a blank piece of paper or in your self-reflective journal, just take a moment to write down how many of the symptoms from the previous list you recognise in yourself.

You could then categorise these symptoms into 'Physical', 'Mental' and 'Emotional' (there may be some cross-over between the categories).

Finally, I invite you to identify any obvious stressors that have led to each of the symptoms and to see if you can find a simple solution to eliminate them.

For example, you may always be running late for work, which causes you to have a headache throughout the day. A simple way to eliminate the stress would be to set the alarm a little earlier. Another possible way to remove the stressor would be to speak with your boss and ask if it would be possible to change your working hours so that you can come in later, if you really do find mornings difficult.

There may not be a solution to every stressor, but even eliminating a few from your life should lead to an improvement in your symptoms. If there are fewer stressors there is less stress and, therefore, less chance for the undischarged Stress Response to accumulate.

For the person who has experienced trauma, the Stress Response is never turned 'off', which is, as you can reasonably imagine and perhaps have experienced, challenging for the body-mind complex on a whole number of different levels.

Feeling constantly stressed may lead to you becoming disconnected from the present moment, living in a state where you find it difficult to focus and get on with your everyday life. This in turn can lead to more stress and so it becomes a vicious cycle.

TTR: Simple 'Grounding Techniques', practices that bring you back to the present moment, can be a useful way to lower your stress levels, as they take you out of memories of the past or anxieties of the future.

You can use the following exercise to remind you that you are, in fact, in the present and not running from the remembered traumas of the past or the imagined stressors of the future. It's a simple practice of active listening to sounds both near and far:

Exercise:

This exercise is about 'grounding', helping you to come back to the present moment when you feel anxious or encounter a triggering situation.

When you're ready, I invite you to focus on all the sounds that are with you in this moment.

What sounds can you hear close to you? See if you can focus on one particularly dominant noise, perhaps birdsong or traffic noise.

Then, once you have established which sounds are close by you in this moment, I invite you to extend your senses further afield and see if you can notice the sounds that are present in the distance.

If you feel comfortable, perhaps you would like to close your eyes and focus on the sounds that are far away.

Then return again to the sounds that are close by.

Paying attention to the sounds that are with you right now, in this present moment, continue with this exercise for as long as you feel comfortable to do so and repeat as often as is necessary for you.

CHAPTER FOUR

UNDERSTANDING TRAUMA

Defining 'Trauma'

'Trauma' is a difficult term to define.

For a start, 'trauma' will mean different things to different people, as we discussed in the last chapter.

We should also try to be clear in differentiating between the experience of suffering from a set of symptoms (e.g. PTS or PTSD/ PTSI) as a result of being exposed to a traumatic event and the traumatic event itself.

The definitions that I give below are *my* definitions. They are categories that I determined from my own understanding of trauma. Some experts may well disagree with the definitions that I use.

When using the word 'trauma' I think that we could be talking about one (or more) of these three things:

1. Experiential trauma: A negative, deeply disturbing or catastrophic event outside of the sphere of normal day-to-day experience.

2. Psychological and physiological trauma: The resultant psychological and comorbid physiological symptoms that an individual suffers as a result of a negative, deeply disturbing or catastrophic experience outside of the sphere of their normal day-to-day experience.

3. Physical trauma: A severe injury to living tissue caused by an extrinsic agent.

'Trauma' may, of course, refer to all three of these definitions at once, as in a soldier severely wounded during combat and suffering from PTSD/PTSI as a result. The circumstances that led up to the injury would be the 'event' (definition 1), the wound would be considered a physical trauma (definition 3) and the PTSD/ PTSI the soldier experiences following the incident is the 'symptom' of trauma (definition 2).

In this book I have tried to make it clear when I am talking about trauma as an event and trauma as a set of symptoms.

The list below is representative, but not exhaustive, of some examples of traumatic events that individuals may encounter in the modern world. If you think that reading this might be a triggering experience for you, please do feel free to skip over it.

Trauma symptoms can be caused by:

- *Bereavement*

- *A life-changing event or injury*

- *War (as either a civilian or a combatant)*

- *Miscarriage*

- *Physical assault*

- *Sexual assault*

- *Rape*

- *Natural disasters*

- *Human trafficking*

- *Child abuse*

- *Mugging*

- *A traffic accident*

- *Acts of terrorism*

- *Financial difficulties*

- *Homelessness*

- Divorce

- Illness

- Chronic or accumulated stress

It's ok if your event isn't on there. I simply want to demonstrate how impossible it is for human beings to avoid trauma entirely.

If you don't experience one kind of trauma, you will likely experience another. You may even experience multiple traumas throughout your life.

The key thing to identify and remember here is that trauma is exclusively caused by a loss of control on the part of the victim.

Whether it's through a natural disaster or constant pressure from work that you can't escape, because you have a mortgage and five kids, the actual mechanism that causes you to become traumatised is the fact that you have lost your agency. Someone or something (or many somethings) have taken away your ability to control an identifiable moment in your past or your day-to-day life.

The way that we can move towards healing the symptoms of trauma is to give ourselves choice and power over our own destiny.

Choice is the key.

By making even one single choice, you've moved yourself just one teeny tiny step closer to healing. Even if that simply means choosing to have a cheese sandwich today instead of a tuna one, you've taken back some of your sense of agency.

It's a sad truism that survivors of trauma may find a simple decision, such as choosing what they want for lunch, to be overwhelming. All of the exercises and techniques offered to you in this book are designed to help you become more comfortable in making choices for yourself.

There are other factors that influence the impact of traumatic events upon an individual:

1. If the event is <u>unexpected</u>, as in the case of a sudden tsunami or physical assault, for instance, you're more likely to suffer symptoms in the body-mind complex.

2. If you are exposed to the <u>accumulation</u> of many traumas, the body-mind complex will eventually reach a point at which it can take no more without exhibiting symptoms.

We'll talk a little more about accumulated and unexpected trauma (often known as Complex Trauma) later on.

So, now we know what trauma symptoms might have been caused by, what are some of these indicators?

You might want to see if you recognise any of the emotional and physical symptoms on this list:

- *Shock, denial, disbelief*

- *Insomnia or nightmares*

- *Anger, irritability, mood swings*

- *Being easily startled*

- *Guilt, shame, self-blame*

- *Racing heartbeat*

- *Feeling sad or hopeless*

- *Aches and pains*

- *Confusion*

- *Fatigue*

- *Difficulty concentrating*

- *Edginess and agitation*

- *Anxiety and fear*

- *Having tense muscles*

- *Becoming socially withdrawn*

- *Feeling disconnected or numb*

As I hope that you can see, being exposed to a traumatic event can cause a number of less than desirable effects within our body-mind complex.

If you're experiencing some or all of these symptoms, it doesn't necessarily mean that you have developed PTSD/ PTSI, but it's probably a good idea to pay a visit to your GP or a mental health professional or to make a trusted friend or loved one aware of what is going on, if you haven't done so already.

Even if you do decide to try out the practices I describe in this book, it's important to give yourself other avenues of support, so that you have many options and many choices available to help you during your recovery.

It should then be easier for you to decide which routes are the most suitable for you and to use your agency to make the choices that best support your own healing.

> *TTR: Choice is vitally important to recovery from trauma and the key to lessening the symptoms that you live with as a trauma survivor.*

The exercise that follows is all about exploring possibilities and choice on a very basic level. It may not have previously occurred to you that decision making could be so simple, so I invite you to try this short exercise now and to notice whether or not your capacity for choice might be able to expand as a result:

Exercise:

When you are ready, you might like to find a shape for your body that feels comfortable to you. You could be sitting or you could be standing. You could choose to lie down on your back or perhaps you prefer to be on your side.

Whatever shape feels comfortable for you, I invite you to take a few moments to find it now.

Once in your shape, see if you can notice any muscles that aren't engaged in this moment. Perhaps your jaw is at rest or maybe your thigh. If you like, see if you can notice what it feels like when a muscle is relaxed.

Perhaps you could now experiment with your shape and see if you can make small changes to it that will allow other muscles to rest.

What does it feel like when your muscles aren't engaged?

Does positioning your arm or your leg or your hand or any other body part differently result in a more restful or less restful shape for you?

I invite you to experiment with these small movements and the resulting sensations for as long as the exercise feels comfortable for you.

CURRENT APPROACHES TOWARDS IDENTIFYING AND TREATING TRAUMA

I'm not going to say too much about these methods (mostly because I'm not an expert), but here is a brief list of the ways in which trauma can be tackled. I'm writing from the UK, but I'm aware that there are different treatment pathways available in other countries.

The main interventions/ therapies available, in no particular order of preference, for UK based trauma survivors are:

1. TRiM – Trauma Risk Management is an initial intervention following a traumatic event as immediately as possible. It's a form of triage that helps practitioners to identify individuals who are at high risk of going on to develop symptoms following trauma and to refer them appropriately. At the same time it acts as an ongoing support practice for those who have experienced trauma, but are not showing signs of high risk behaviours. TRiM is a peer-to-peer management practice and therein lays its greatest strength.

2. CBT – Cognitive Behavioural Therapy is a talk therapy that can help individuals to manage their symptoms, following trauma, by changing the way that they think and behave.

3. EMDR - Eye Movement Desensitisation and Reprocessing is a form of psychotherapy that uses eye movements and other forms of bilateral stimulation to assist individuals in processing traumatic memories and beliefs.

4. Talk Therapy – This involves speaking with a counsellor or other mental health professional about the traumatic event/ events. It may involve direct discussion of the event itself, but is more likely to cover the thoughts and feelings that an individual is left with following their traumatic experience. These sessions are usually survivor led in terms of the content that is discussed, but the counsellor or other mental health professional may offer guidance or 'homework' for the survivor to work on.

5. TIR – Traumatic Incident Reduction Therapy involves repeated revisiting of the traumatic memory under supervised conditions. The therapist doesn't offer any interpretation or evaluation of the incident.

6. Pharmacological Interventions - Most commonly used are SSRIs, (Selective Serotonin Reuptake Inhibitors) including fluoxetine (Prozac), sertraline and paroxetine. There's much debate over the efficacy of using medication to treat the symptoms of trauma.

7. Complementary/ Alternative Therapies - The Arts, Animal Assisted Therapy (AAT), acupuncture, massage, aromatherapy, Yoga, meditation and mindfulness are all considered to fall into this category.

As you can see, some of these approaches have features in common, others are wildly different. Often a combination of these interventions is the most appropriate way for an individual to move towards healing and I encourage you to explore which pathways may be most effective for you. It may take some time and a measure of trial and error to find the combination that is most effective and appropriate for your needs, but perseverance and acknowledging when a treatment is or isn't working for you is the key to this process.

Complementary/ Alternative therapies, as the name suggests, are often a useful adjunct and can support survivors receiving another form of intervention. They are also effective self-help tools that can help you to help yourself in between appointments and other treatments. You may also discover, as I did, that complementary therapies are the most effective long-term management tools, as they aren't dependent upon an external facilitator and can evolve according to your changing needs.

Below is an alternative technique that's useful both for grounding and for helping the body to relax. It's called Progressive Relaxation:

Exercise:

When we feel stressed, we hold onto that emotion inside our bodies, particularly within the muscles. Progressive Relaxation works by first tensing the muscles (one at a time) and then consciously allowing them to relax.

If you'd like to try it, all you have to do is sit or lay down somewhere comfortable. You might want to take your shoes off too.

When you feel ready to begin, I invite you to focus your attention on your right foot and to see if you can notice any sensations there.

Then, you might like to experiment with slowly tensing up all of the muscles in your right foot, holding for as long as feels comfortable to you (maybe 10 seconds or less if that feels too much) and then relax your foot again when you are ready.

You might want to take a moment to notice how your right foot feels now, before moving on to the other muscle groups in your body.

You could use this sequence (or you could make up your own)

- *Right foot*

- *Left foot*

- *Right calf*

- *Left calf*

- *Right thigh*

- *Left thigh*

- *Hips and gluteal muscles*

- *Stomach*

- *Chest*

- Back

- Right hand

- Right arm

- Left hand

- Left arm

- Shoulders

- Neck

- Face

When you've gone through each muscle group, you might've noticed that some areas felt more tense than others or that the exercise was particularly soothing for some muscle groups. You may not have noticed much difference and that's OK too.

You might want to just take a moment after you have finished, to just breathe at your own pace and ground yourself, before resuming your usual activities.

You can do this exercise as often as you like, if you found it helpful.

CHAPTER SIX

POST TRAUMATIC STRESS (PTS) AND POST TRAUMATIC STRESS DISORDER/ INJURY (PTSD/PTSI)

Sometimes an event is too traumatic, too unexpected or our resiliency is so low, that the feelings, emotions and bodily sensations generated by an experience are too overwhelming for the body-mind complex to absorb, even after the event itself is long over. The body is unable to store the memory/ memories away in the filing cabinets of the brain as it usually would, which leads to them and/ or the feelings associated with them resurfacing at unexpected moments (a flashback) or when similar circumstances remind you of what you experienced (a trigger).

TTR: A flashback is a vivid experience, during which you relive some or all of the aspects of a traumatic event or feel as though it is happening to you again in the present moment. A flashback may be experienced through physical sensations, emotions or visualisation.

This is the basic physiological mechanism that people experience during Post Traumatic Stress (PTS). If the trauma doesn't integrate and the memories remain 'unfiled' for an extended period of time, Post Traumatic Stress Disorder/ Injury (PTSD/ PTSI) may be diagnosed.

Put simply, PTS and PTSD/ PTSI are caused by the brain functioning differently to the way it does in an untraumatised person.

Note here, the brain isn't *damaged*.

It's just operating in a *different* way.

You are *not* broken.

TTR: A trigger can be physical, emotional or mental. You might hear a sound that reminds you of one you heard during a traumatic event or some circumstance might lead you to feel the same way you did during a traumatic event. Triggers are sometimes easy to identify (e.g.

fireworks reminding a soldier of shots being fired or explosions), but aren't always obvious.

It can be helpful to make a note of things that you recognise as obvious triggers, so that you can prepare yourself for them in advance or choose to avoid them completely.

Essentially, the person suffering from PTS or PTSD/PTSI has reverted to the more primitive way of functioning that is necessary for the human organism to survive in the face of extreme danger, assessing everything that they encounter in day-to-day life as an extreme threat. The higher functioning areas of the brain (the midline structures) are 'shutdown' or 'bypassed', so that the person is not able to objectively evaluate what they are seeing, hearing, smelling or feeling.

The brain and body become stuck in the protective fight-flight-freeze-flop response, unable to switch it off, and so the person suffering from PTS or PTSD/PTSI finds it difficult to relax and function within the normal parameters of their personality.

Additionally, all human beings have an inbuilt negativity bias, a primal response designed to protect us without us having to waste the time analysing whether or not something is a threat. A good example of this is seeing a piece of rope in bad light and thinking that it looks like a snake. So, rather than us having to step on it to find out whether or not it will bite us, we automatically avoid it. For the person suffering from PTS or PTSD/ PTSI this negativity bias is constantly activated, which may lead to catastrophising, depression and anxiety.

To summarise, some common symptoms of PTSD/ PTSI might include:

- Re-experiencing the traumatic event; through flashbacks, nightmares, memories or intense emotional or physical reactions when reminded of the trauma.

- Avoidance; avoiding places, activities, thoughts or feelings that remind you of the trauma.

- Emotional numbing; inability to remember aspects of the event, loss of interest in previously enjoyable activities and general daily life, feeling detached from others or emotionally numb, feeling as though your future is limited.

- Hyperalertness; difficulty falling or staying asleep, difficulty concentrating, hypervigilance, feeling jumpy or being easily startled.

- Other; anger and irritability, shame, guilt or self-blame, substance misuse, depression, suicidal thoughts and feelings, feeling alienated

*and alone, lack of trust, physical symptoms like
headaches, stomach problems or chest pains.*

It's unsurprising, given the physiological processes in play, that people suffering from PTS or PTSD/ PTSI exhibit behaviour that may appear extreme to the people around them.

TTR: If you are experiencing PTS or PTSD/ PTSI you are NOT BROKEN!

I can't stress strongly enough that everything that a person experiences as a result of trauma is a *perfectly natural and logical response initiated by the body-mind complex to protect itself.*

The body-mind complex is not damaged by trauma (a physical injury obviously being the exception here). It's merely thrown into an instinctual feedback loop that's part of the body-mind's survival toolkit.

If we look at PTS or PTSD/ PTSI from this perspective, we can see that it's actually a 'helpful' condition (even though it obviously doesn't feel this way to the person suffering from it) intended to protect the body-mind complex from the trauma that it has experienced.

We have already explored some simple grounding exercises in previous chapters, below is a longer practice that is integral to Yoga Nidra, which we will explore in more detail later.

For the moment, I invite you to try out 'Body Sensing' and see what you notice about your body-mind complex after you have finished:

> *Exercise:*
>
> *Take a moment now, if you're ready, and bring your attention to your right thumb... to your right index finger... to your right middle finger... to your right ring finger... to your right little finger... feel your whole hand... feel now your right arm... the wrist... the lower arm... the elbow... the upper arm... your right shoulder... the whole of the right arm... your right side, the whole way down the torso... feel the pelvis... bring the attention now to your right leg... to the right thigh... to the right knee... to the right calf... to the right ankle... to your right foot... to the right big toe... to the second toe... to the middle toe... to the fourth toe... to the little toe... feel your entire right side...*
>
> *[Pause]*
>
> *Turn your attention now to your left thumb... to your left index finger... to your left middle finger... to your left ring finger... to your left*

little finger... feel your whole hand... feel now your left arm... the wrist... the lower arm... the elbow... the upper arm... your left shoulder... the whole of the left arm... your left side, the whole way down the torso... feel the pelvis... bring the attention now to your left leg... to the left thigh... to the left knee... to the left calf... to the left ankle... to your left foot... to the left big toe... to the second toe... to the middle toe... to the fourth toe... to the little toe... feel your entire left side...

[Pause]

Feel the throat and the sensations that are there... Now focus on the mouth... the sensations inside the mouth... the tongue... the lips... the plane between the lips, where they don't touch... bring your awareness to your nose... to your right eyebrow... the orbit of your right eye... the left eyebrow... the orbit of your left eye... feel the inside of the right ear... the outside of the right ear... the inside of the left ear... the outside of the left ear... feel both ears together... feel the whole face together... feel the entire head...

Feel your entire right hand... feel your entire left hand... feel both hands together... feel your right foot... feel your left foot... feel both feet together... feel both ankles together... feel both knees together... feel the pelvis and both hips together... feel the abdomen... feel the chest... feel the right shoulder... feel the left shoulder... feel both shoulders together... feel both elbows together... feel both wrists together... feel both hands together... feel the entire body, leaving nothing out... feel everything from the crown of the head to the very tips of the toes... feel the entire body... feel the entire body...

You can repeat this rotation of awareness as many times as you feel you need to ground you firmly in the present and bring you back out of your triggered memory.

If you wanted to, you could record yourself reading this short script (perhaps on your phone or another device you often carry with you) and play it back whenever you felt the need. You could also simply memorise the sections that you find most helpful, perhaps just focusing on the hands for example, and use this as a way to anchor yourself in the present moment.

This practice of Body Sensing is a very effective way of bringing you back into the present and encouraging the body-mind complex to relax.

It's best to start with the hands, because they take up the largest proportion of the cortical homunculus (a way of representing the parts of the brain dedicated to processing motor functions and sensory functions for different parts of the body) and allows you to more easily trigger the release of muscular and emotional tension.

If you do nothing else when Body Sensing, you can just focus on the hands, one finger at a time and repeat this process until you feel the memory of your trauma fading and sense yourself rooted firmly back in the present moment.

Whilst it may be difficult to master this technique the first few times that you're triggered, as you become more familiar with your experiences and what is likely to trigger you, you can even begin Body Sensing before the triggering event happens.

For instance:

> *I know that unknown people walking behind me is a particular trigger of mine, due to the nature of my traumatic experience. If I'm out in public where I know that people are going to be walking behind me, on the Tube in London or whilst out shopping, I bring my attention to my right thumb and focus it there. I then move on to the other fingers on my right hand and*

then do the same with my left hand. I keep repeating this rotation backwards and forwards until I feel more at ease.

I approach triggers with an attitude of non-judgement. I don't treat myself harshly if I need to use Body Sensing, which is an extension of the Loving-Kindness exercise that we practised earlier on in the book.

If you are able to approach your triggers with less fear and resentment, then you are likely to respond with more kindness to yourself and the people around you. If you feel more in control of your body-mind complex during and after a trigger, then it's easier to approach your triggers in this way.

TTR: Please treat yourself gently and respectfully, it's what your body-mind complex deserves!

CHAPTER SEVEN

COMPLEX TRAUMA

Complex Trauma (also known as Complex PTSD/ cPTSD) can be diagnosed in both adults and children who have repeatedly experienced traumatic events, which may include violence, neglect or abuse. It may also be diagnosed if the traumatic event happened suddenly or if you were alone during the experience.

Here's a summary of the primary causes of Complex Trauma:

- *A traumatic event that happened early in life (during childhood and the formative years).*

- *Trauma inflicted by a parent or carer (someone that you should've been able to trust).*

> *- Experiencing the trauma for a long time (repeated abuse or neglect, for example).*
>
> *- Being alone during the traumatic event (during a rape, a natural disaster, a mugging etc.).*
>
> *- The survivor still being in contact with the person who caused the trauma (e.g. an abusive family member who has never been 'outed').*

Complex Trauma is a tricky condition to live with and to diagnose, due to that fact that the symptoms it causes are not always triggered by one exclusive and readily identifiable event. Where Complex Trauma is caused by an identifiable event, such as sexual assault, the survivor often feels shame or guilt and won't talk about what happened. This secrecy is another initiator of Complex Trauma and can also be a barrier to its resolution and diagnosis.

If the Complex Trauma was caused by an accumulation of events or an event that you haven't acknowledged due to feelings of shame, it's harder to determine what situations you will find triggering and harder for clinicians to identify what led to your symptoms in the first instance.

It can take many, many years for the symptoms of Complex Trauma to be recognised. This means that the survivor's development and behaviour may be influenced by it as they get older or that they may be less responsive to conventional trauma treatments, because there is no single isolated incident to be resolved.

To add another layer of complication to our understanding of the development of Complex Trauma, to a large extent an individual's level of resilience determines how susceptible they will be not only to the after-effects of any trauma, but specifically how likely they are to develop Complex Trauma.

One's level of resilience is, by its very nature, commonly lowered by experiencing trauma during one's formative years, which is why so many sufferers of childhood abuse go on to develop Complex Trauma.

Similarly, repeated exposure to trauma or chronic stress lowers resiliency, which again can lead to the development of Complex Trauma.

We will explore resiliency in more detail in the next chapter.

However, all of this having been said, yogic approaches can be very helpful indeed for assisting with Complex Trauma symptoms, as is evidenced by the work of David Emerson at the Trauma Center and Dr. Richard Miller of the Integrative Restoration Institute (see bibliography for references to their work). This is because Trauma Informed Yoga (TIY), in any form, targets the effects of trauma within the body and gently asks you to return to the present, without demanding that you relive or even acknowledge your trauma.

The theory goes that by healing the body from the effects of trauma, we are able to heal the mind, as the body-mind complex is inseparable. What you do to the body, you do to the mind and vice versa.

Below is another simple grounding exercise for you to try, if you like.

My aim with this book is to give you variety and to facilitate choice, so I invite you to choose which exercises you like best and to discard those that you don't find quite so helpful.

Exercise:

This exercise is about connecting you with the physical sensation of being in the present moment.

You could use it to support you during a triggering situation or simply to help you to connect with the present in your day-to-day life.

If you are standing and it's comfortable and safe to do so, I invite you to remove your shoes and socks. If you like, take a moment now to feel the soles of the feet connecting with the floor. See if you can notice any sensations in the soles of your feet and the pads of the toes.

I invite you to stand tall, with your shoulders slightly back and down, your chest expanded and your chin lifted. Your hands can rest comfortably by your sides.

I invite you to feel your connection with the floor, with the Earth, and to notice any sensations within the feet and the legs.

If there are no sensations for you, that's OK too and you can simply acknowledge the lack of sensation and see if this changes for you at any point during the exercise.

I invite you to stay here as long as it feels comfortable for you, simply noticing the place where the soles of your feet make contact with the floor and any physical sensations that arise (or not) as a result.

CHAPTER EIGHT

CHRONIC STRESS AND RESILIENCE

As mentioned in the previous chapter, trauma symptoms, and also the onset of Complex Trauma, are not always caused by a single catastrophic event. Sometimes an accumulation of stress simply creeps up on the unwary as an unwelcome result of the lifestyle that many of us lead and this can result in the same physical and mental symptoms as one might expect to experience following a major traumatic event.

Most people living in the modern (Western) world now experience chronic stress simply as a result of daily living.

We're always 'switched on', always connected.

We live in a 24-hour culture, where people are constantly exposed to social media and its associated pressures.

People are always available.

We can receive work emails, often directly to our smart phones, even when we're at home, and rarely do we take the time to calm down and step away from our commitments.

How many times in a day do you turn everything off (actually *off*, not just on silent) and simply sit and just be?

Do you know how many times each hour you check your phone or emails or social media channels?

We're encouraged to sleep less and work more, to always strive for and to set new goals.

We take caffeine to wake us up and drink alcohol or pop pills to send us to sleep.

Our self-esteem is tied to external appearance and conspicuous consumption.

We no longer prize real-life interactions and our sense of community has eroded to the extent that it's virtually non-existent.

It's little wonder, therefore, that people are increasingly suffering from burnout, mental breakdowns and addiction problems.

TTR: You are a human being, not a human doing.

People have become less resilient due to the constant and insidious pressures of the culture that we, in the West, champion and, as a direct result, we are more vulnerable than ever to the negative effects of trauma and cumulative stress.

I invite you to try the exercise below and see if you can identify the stressors in your life.

You may be surprised by how these minor stressors soon add up to quite a long list and how many hours of your day they can come to consume:

Exercise:

Take a moment now, if you want to, to make another list.

Try to recall and write down all the distractions that arise during your typical day.

The list should include things like:

- mobile phones

- laptops

- tablets

- TVs

- emails

- messaging services

- social media

- news updates

- demanding colleagues

- family members (e.g. children)

- pets (e.g. your dog that has to be walked)

- chores (household or otherwise)

- deadlines

- commuting

- To Do lists

It may be pretty obvious now that you actually have very little space left just to be yourself after you've dealt with all these things that demand your attention.

Resilience

As we have discussed in previous chapters, what will be considered traumatic for by person won't be by another. One person may sail easily through a divorce or the loss of their job, whereas another may find either of these events traumatic enough to trigger stress-related symptoms. The extent to which an individual will be traumatised by any given experience is largely dependent upon their resilience.

If our resilience is being steadily eroded by the constant pressures and minor stressors of modern day living, when we actually *do* face a traumatic event of significant proportions we have little left mentally and physically to help us through the experience.

Resilience can be defined as the ability to adapt effectively and to recover from disappointment, difficulty or crisis. It's determined by lots of factors, both external (mostly stuff you can't control) and internal (this stuff is almost totally in your hands).

External factors include, but aren't limited to:

- *Family background (the type of family in which you were raised and their expectations and values).*

- *School life (what type of school you go/ went to and where, as well as your own day-to-day experience of school).*

- *Community (the wider community in which you live).*

- *Peer support (people in your social group).*

Internal factors may include, but aren't limited to:

- *Your attitudes (are you generally cheerful or do you approach everything with disdain, distrust or apathy?).*

> *- Your perceptions (do you think the world is for you or against you? Do you feel like you can trust others or do you feel like you can't?).*
>
> *- Your behaviours (do you engage in healthy behaviours, such as regular exercise and meditation, or do you engage in negative behaviours, such as smoking and drinking heavily?).*

You have very little control over external factors, but almost complete control over internal factors.

Some of your internal factors may have been shaped by external factors, such as experiencing interpersonal trauma and so believing you can't trust anyone, but you *can* choose to challenge and modify your own beliefs.

You can help to strengthen your internal factors by developing protective factors that help to build your resiliency.

Protective factors include, but aren't limited to:

> *- Standing up for what you believe in; believe in something or fall for anything.*
>
> *- Being authentic/ honest with yourself; do you really want to go to Aunt Susie's birthday party or meet the guys from the office for karaoke?*

- *Resisting negative peer pressure; no you don't need to smoke that joint or have another drink just because your friends do.*

- *Developing a sense of purpose; even if this is just catching up with your favourite TV series on Netflix or reading a good book.*

- *Developing a positive outlook about your future; believing that everything will be OK and that you can live your best life.*

Unfortunately, because not all of the factors that influence resiliency are under our control, some people are made more vulnerable to trauma than others.

Please be warned, the following example may be triggering for some, but hopefully it will demonstrate the interaction between resiliency, internal/ external factors and vulnerability to suffering the symptoms of trauma:

Let's consider the example of a child who has suffered abuse.

A child who has grown up in an unstable home or one who has experienced abuse from a young age will be negatively impacted by these external factors, but, in addition, will also have limited capacity to develop their internal factors and supporting protective factors.

Such a child may then grow into an adult who believes that they are worthless or damaged or they may develop a negative world-view.

As an adult, a relatively minor traumatic experience could then be enough to create severe psychological and physiological symptoms, perhaps even leading to PTSD/ PTSI.

However, extensive trauma doesn't always lead to lowered resilience. Sometimes it has the opposite effect.

We will look at this in more detail in the chapter on Post Traumatic Growth (PTG) later on.

Generally, though, it's accurate and appropriate to say that the way that a trauma affects us is dependent upon our level of resilience.

If you like, you could have a go at the following exercise to help you think about your own level of resilience and the changes that you could make to increase your protective factors:

Exercise:

If you like, use a blank piece of paper (or your self-reflective journal) to write down a list of your external factors, then your internal factors and finally your protective factors.

You may realise, during this process, that some of your external factors were not particularly helpful for developing resiliency.

By realising this, you may now be able to challenge some of your internal factors and, so, strengthen some of your protective factors.

Example:

External Factor - You were abused as a child.

Internal Factor – Your attitude is one of cynicism, mistrust and disdain.

Protective Factor – You decide to develop a more positive outlook, after realising that your past is in the past and, as a result, develop a sense of purpose that leads you to start a charity that helps others who have experienced abuse during childhood.

Hopefully the exercise above helped you to understand a little bit more about yourself. Maybe it has given you a few ideas about the things that you could do to improve your level of resiliency and so reduce the effects of experiencing trauma in your life.

For me, the biggest part of healing myself was *understanding* myself and deciding what actions I could take that would help me to develop my protective factors and become a more resilient person. This process naturally led to me becoming happier, healthier and more fulfilled, so that I added more protective factors to my arsenal of defences and continued to strengthen my resilience.

See what I'm getting at here?

It's a cycle:

> *TTR: Increase your resilience = increase your happiness = lessen the negative effects of trauma = increased resilience = increased happiness = lessened negative effects of trauma.*

The last stage in this process, during which you experience greater happiness and are less affected by traumatic events/ symptoms, would be termed 'Post Traumatic Growth' (PTG); becoming more than you were before the traumatic event, rather than being diminished by it.

We will look at PTG in the next chapter

.

POST TRAUMATIC GROWTH (PTG)

Post Traumatic Growth is a term that's used to refer to positive changes that an individual might experience following a traumatic event.

There is a theory that people will intrinsically move towards growth following adversity, because the experience of trauma leads to a breakdown of the beliefs that formed our previous identity. This breakdown is signalled by the onset of symptoms of PTS or PTSD/PTSI.

Consequently, working through PTS or PTSD/ PTSI may become a catalyst to PTG, which allows you to rebuild yourself in a way that maximises your psychological wellbeing.

TTR: "What doesn't kill you makes you stronger." Friedrich Nietzsche

Many people find that, as a result of surviving a traumatic experience, their priorities in life change and they come to appreciate the positives in life, whilst more easily dismissing the negatives.

Trauma can be a great way to shine a spotlight onto our lives and to really see ourselves clearly for the first time.

Although all traumatic events are unpleasant by their very nature, it doesn't mean that some good can't come out of having survived the experience.

A Hierarchy of Needs

During and immediately following trauma, the body-mind complex is primarily occupied with surviving. It cares only about the basic physiological needs of the body. The fight-flight-freeze-flop response is necessary in many situations to preserve the life of the person during the traumatic experience (e.g. a firefight or being chased by a pack of hungry wolves).

The body works only to preserve its basic needs and to keep the body-mind complex alive.

These needs generally include things like; escaping from danger, seeking shelter, keeping warm, feeding ourselves, excreting waste, staying awake and alert.

All the basic stuff you need to do in order to remain a viable human organism in the face of extreme threat.

Once the trauma is over, the symptoms that remain are no longer useful for meeting our basic needs and can, in fact, compromise these (e.g. hyperalertness that prevents us from sleeping).

In order for human beings to live full and meaningful lives they must be able to do more than merely survive.

Humans need to stimulate their imagination and express curiousity, but, as we already discussed, because the midline structures of the brain (that control imagination and higher level thinking) go offline during a traumatic experience, we have to find ways to switch these back on and to cultivate emotional, mental and spiritual growth.

I'm going to talk more about curiousity later in this book, but it's important to note here that Darwin identified what he called the 'curiousity muscle' as early as 1872. This is the sternocleidomastoid muscle that runs down either side of your neck. When we are traumatised or melancholy, we tend to keep our heads down and don't engage this muscle at all. When we are feeling positive, happy and curious, our whole shape changes and this muscle becomes active.

Yoga *asana* is great, because it improves our shape and encourages us to engage this muscle. This is why I'm a fan of backbends and upright shapes, rather than forward folds, which encourage us to drop our heads and disengage our curiousity about external stimulus (more on this later).

In order to undergo PTG we must become curious about the world around us once more and, by becoming curious, we open ourselves up to the possibilities of choice and change that lead to our personal growth and development.

Areas of PTG

Academic studies have identified five key areas that are indicative of PTG:

1. You become a stronger person: you are more capable of handling stressors following your recovery from trauma.

2. You become closer to people: you value the people in your life who support and nurture you and invest more time in cultivating these relationships.

3. You appreciate everything: you wake up each day feeling happy to be alive and no longer sweat the little things.

4. You are open to new opportunities: you realise that you can do and be anything that you want, because you have experienced possibly the worst thing that you ever will and so you are no longer afraid to be who or what you want to be.

5. You realise that life is perhaps more than just this body-mind complex: you begin to explore new spiritual possibilities, perhaps even to the extent of experiencing an epiphany or spiritual awakening.

Resiliency and Post Traumatic Growth

Inversely, in contrast to our earlier discussion about those with a lower level of resiliency being more likely to experience PTSD/ PTSI, people who begin with a higher base level of resiliency are in fact *less* likely to experience PTG than those who have a low level of resiliency before experiencing trauma.

If you've had some really terrible experiences in your life and you generally feel fairly hacked off, the chances are that your resiliency is low and therefore you actually have the most potential to experience PTG.

To summarise; a positive outcome of PTG is higher resilience, but an outcome of higher initial resilience is a lower level of PTG.

The following exercise is about PTG. I invite you to try it, if you like, and to see if you can identify some areas in which you have already experienced PTG or other areas in which you might like to:

Exercise:

If you like, draw out a table on a piece of paper or in your self-reflective journal.

On one side you can put the numbers 1-5, referring back to the areas of PTG identified above.

On the other side you can think about how these areas relate to your life and if you have, in fact, grown in any of them since experiencing your trauma.

If the answer is 'no', perhaps you might like to identify some areas in which you would like to grow.

It can sometimes be quite fruitful, after you've been practicing yoga regularly for a while, to revisit this exercise and to see whether or not your answers are still the same.

You may find that you have some surprising and rather pleasing results.

CHAPTER TEN

YOGIC PERSPECTIVES ON TRAUMA

Yogis believe that 'trauma' (the experience) is an undischarged energy event that affects the body-mind complex on all levels, even long after the event itself has actually passed.

When the traumatic event is buried, rather than faced, we develop an energy knot, a *granthi*, which is basically like a massive sludgeberg that has blocked the pipes of your kitchen sink (you and your body-mind complex being the metaphorical sink and its pipes). When you experience ordinary life stuff, because this sludgeberg hasn't been removed, you continue to put more washing-up water and bits of food waste on top of it, until, eventually, the sink overflows.

This cascade of detritus is formed of the symptoms that you suffer with on a day-to-day basis (flashbacks, nightmares, dissociation, hyperalertness etc.). If you keep trying to run more water down that blocked plughole, you're only going to make the flood worse.

What we need to do, then, is get out a plunger (ideally before our body-mind complex turns into sludgeville) and clear that nasty wad of grime, so that it no longer blocks our pipes.

However, if you've already got to the stage of sink catastrophe, I'm afraid that the only way for normal drainage function to resume is to wade through that murky water and get your hands dirty. The dirt, of course, being the emotions, sensations and thoughts related to the traumatic incident that has caused such a backlog and the job of removing that sludge falling to the yogic-plunger.

In order for you to move forwards that troublesome, pipe-blocking, sludgeberg has to go!

Stress, Trauma and The Koshas

So, pipe metaphors aside, trauma itself, in yogic terms, is merely an expression of energy. Everything that we experience in our lives is an energetic event, which we feel as various sensations throughout the body-mind complex. These sensations can be physical, emotional and mental.

On this point, both yoga and science pretty much agree, but in yoga theory, this is explained by the Koshas (we will look at these in even more detail later), rather than by neuroscience:

> - *Anna Maya Kosha:* expresses physical symptoms (e.g. aches and pains, tension headaches, fatigue, muscle tension).
>
> - *Prana Maya Kosha:* expresses energy body symptoms (e.g. shallow breathing, arrhythmic, uneven breathing, tiredness).
>
> - *Mano Maya Kosha:* expresses psychological symptoms (e.g. feeling edgy and nervous, anger, apathy, fear, guilt, shame).
>
> - *Vijnana Maya Kosha:* expresses belief symptoms (e.g. feeling unworthy, as though the world is against you, low self-esteem, grief, the inability to forgive or love).
>
> - *Ananda Maya Kosha:* expresses the inability to access this Kosha (i.e. never feeling joyful and at ease with oneself).

Now that you know a little bit about the Koshas, you might like to try the exercise below:

> *Exercise:*

Now could be a time to start thinking about your own symptoms and putting them into categories.

Where are you feeling your sludgeberg the most?

Is it in the Mano Maya Kosha (the mind)?

Or is it in the Anna Maya Kosha (the body)?

I invite you to make a table with the Koshas on one side and to see if you can fit the symptoms that you are experiencing into the category of a particular Kosha.

This table will help you to determine which areas your yoga practice particularly needs to target in order to provide relief.

You may well find that you have problems in several or all of the Koshas. This is perfectly normal and fine. It just means that you get to do more yoga.

Lucky you!

Integration

If the energy load created by the experience of trauma is allowed to follow its natural course through the body-mind complex, the sensations are felt, experienced and then integrated.

For instance, after an animal has become stressed or scared, you will often see it physically shake to release the tension. This is a protective mechanism that allows immediate integration of the trauma to occur and prevents the animal from developing a blockage.

Integration, on a practical level, means that the experience (whether positive or negative) has been filed away into memory by the mind and can be recounted without any negative physical, emotional or psychological sensations.

The mind is the key to this process, which is why yoga, Yoga Nidra and other meditation/ mindfulness practices are focused on either quieting or controlling the movements of the monkey mind.

When the body-mind complex experiences an event that is too intense, overwhelming or frequent for it to process (whether that event is seen, heard, felt or all three), it can't clear the energy and the event cannot be integrated.

This is when the body-mind complex becomes overwhelmed and the normal nervous system response is shut down in order for us to survive the event.

However, because the energy was not integrated during the event, it remains in the body-mind complex for us to come back to and process at a later time, when we feel safer and more able to do so.

If we have experienced a relatively minor trauma and we have a high level of resilience, the energy created may be integrated when the mind-body complex has had a chance to recover and revisit the experience in a safe space (this is basically what talk therapy is designed to do).

> *TTR: The Third Law of Thermodynamics, which says; "Energy is neither created nor destroyed, it simply changes form."*

Complementary/ alternative therapies, such as Trauma Informed Yoga, can allow us to revisit the trauma in a less challenging, more indirect way, in our own space and time and so allow us to heal even when conventional therapies have failed.

Complementary/alternative therapies, as the name suggests, can also provide an excellent complement to existing therapies that you are pursuing and you shouldn't forsake your existing treatment plan in favour of a yogic one.

Yogic perspectives on trauma may, however, allow you to understand your situation in a different way and help you to experience the positive effects of PTG.

CHAPTER ELEVEN

THE RELAXATION RESPONSE

Turning Stress 'Off'

In order to bring the body-mind complex to a place where PTG can occur, we need to 'switch-off' the Stress Response. The easiest and most effective way to do this is to trigger the Relaxation Response.

The Relaxation Response was first documented by Herbert Benson, MD, in the 1960s at Harvard Medical School (see the bibliography for details).

The Relaxation Response utilises the parasympathetic nervous system and has the effect of:

- *Turning the Stress Response off.*

- *Normalising stress hormone levels.*

- Regulating the heart rate and pulse to healthy levels.

- Lowering high blood pressure.

- Slowing the respiratory rate and decreasing oxygen consumption.

- Decreasing muscle tension.

- Increasing blood flow to major muscles.

- Reducing fatigue and increasing energy.

Triggering the Relaxation Response usually just generally makes us feel better.

TTR: There is a precaution about the Relaxation Response (detailed in Chapter 12) and its negative effects for a minority of individuals. You might want to have a quick read before trying out the exercise in this chapter.

The Relaxation Response is a powerful antidote to the stresses of our modern lives and to tackling the symptoms of trauma.

Triggering the Relaxation Response doesn't have to be complicated. It can be as simple as trying out the breathing exercise below.

Before trying the exercise, please do bear in mind that some people will be triggered by altering their breathing patterns, so please approach the second part of the exercise with caution (particularly if you are a military veteran, who was trained to link his or her breathing to actions taken when discharging a weapon).

If you feel comfortable and ready to try, then I invite you to give this exercise a go:

Exercise:

The breath is like a sneaky little back-door to the mind and therefore also the body.

If you're panting or breathing in sharp, shallow breaths, the chances are that you're stressed or injured.

Similarly, if your inhales are longer than your exhales, the chances are that you're not a happy bunny.

Take a moment now, if you want to, to just tune in to your breath.

Without trying to change or influence what's going on, see if you can work out what your breath is doing.

If your inhalations and exhalations are regular and deep, that's great - you are likely in a pretty chilled state!

If your breathing is fast and shallow or you have particularly long inhales and short exhales, you might want to try the following breathing pattern, which can be used to calm panic attacks.

<u>7:11 Breath</u>

With a timer or a clock handy (or counting in your head) inhale for the count of seven seconds and then slowly exhale for the count of eleven seconds.

As the exhalation passes the eighth second, you should start to feel some calming effect.

Repeat this 7:11 breath as many times as you like, as long as it feels OK for you.

You might also want to give yourself a little hug as you do it, crossing your arms over your chest.

This way of breathing can also be a good way to send yourself off to sleep if you are struggling with racing thoughts at night.

Hopefully, you can see for yourself that breathing practice and, by extension yoga, has a very sneaky and effective way of triggering the Relaxation Response and making you feel better.

The Relaxation Response is, quite simply, the opposite of the Stress Response and is a useful way of bringing the body-mind complex back to a neutral state.

CHAPTER TWELVE

YOGA BASICS

I'm still not entirely sure why yoga works, but I know that it does for me and that it's been scientifically proven to for others as well (see bibliography for studies).

Yoga has many physical benefits, but it also has a boatload of emotional and mental benefits too. I could list them all below, but I think it's best if you try it out for yourself and see what it does for you.

The thing that I want to make absolutely crystal clear is that this is not a book on How You Must Practice. This is about *your* healing journey and this is totally unique to *you*.

I will explain what I do and how it works for me, as well as giving you some practical advice on how best to avoid injury during *asana*, but the finer nuances of practice are yours to investigate and explore.

You can choose to try out all of the shapes that I use, or not.

Similarly, I have included a sample Yoga Nidra script that I've written and used, but I encourage you to do more reading/ listening in this area and to find (or write) the scripts that work best for you. There are lots of resources to help you do this listed in the bibliography at the end of the book.

The Human Condition

We've already talked about the Koshas, from a yogic perspective and, shortly, we're going to examine them in even more detail. But, first, I'd just like us to reflect for a moment on what it means to be human.

Are we the body?

Are we the mind?

Are we the things we own?

Are we the job that we do?

Yogis believe that five layers (Koshas) hide the Inner Self, otherwise described as our True Nature. Most people incorrectly believe that these five layers make up the entirety of whom and what we are.

This is the illusion referred to as *maya*.

Our Inner Self may also be called the Atma.

The Atma is the source of our transcendental Self (the bit of us that exists outside of the body-mind complex, sometimes called the 'soul' or 'Spirit').

When one accesses the Atma there's a spontaneous and genuine inner knowing and remembrance of the universal consciousness (Atman/ Source) of which we are all part (some people like to think of this as 'God' or the Universe itself).

Atma is realised when we are able to relax into just 'being'.

We feel stressed in our day-to-day lives and out of touch with the Atma because our Inner Self is overshadowed by the Koshas.

The Pursuit of Happiness

The illusion of the Koshas leads us to believe that we are no more than our physical body, so we mistakenly seek out temporary pleasure that gratifies the senses, rather than enduring happiness and joy.

Hey, who doesn't want to eat another tub of delicious ice-cream?

Even though it won't bring us enlightenment it sure can make us seem happy for about five minutes.

Human beings can spend their entire lives seeking and chasing happiness.

But what does it mean to be 'happy'?

Happiness is an elusive concept.

When we imagine experiencing joy, we expect to feel a sense of elation, like winning the lottery, rather than a subtle sense of peacefulness and contentment.

I always use the analogy of falling in love vs. being in love to help explain this difference:

> *When you first meet someone you can't keep your hands off of each other. You both experience limerence, total infatuation. Then, after you've been together for a while, your love deepens and becomes something else entirely, a deep and peaceful contentment with one another and an instinctive and undeniable knowing that you belong together, even when you're just sitting on the sofa together in the evening watching TV.*

The unrealistic expectation of wanting to always feel limerence, which is how we believe 'happiness' should feel, throughout our daily lives clouds our thoughts and feelings and actually, in the end, prevents us from recognising and experiencing true happiness.

This is why people are always seeking more. For example:

That one hit of extreme happiness from buying the new boots we saved so hard for quickly disappears when we realise they are pretty much the same as our old boots and we still have to go to work, pay the mortgage and do the dishes. The new boots didn't really solve anything and we're still basically exactly the same as we were when we were new-bootless.

We're just a bit poorer.

It's far better to seek the security of your comfy old boots, knowing that you've already walked many miles together and that they won't give you blisters; even if they aren't quite so shiny or smooth anymore.

Happiness is then found in the freedom from wanting the new boots, because you are already content with what you have.

The Eternal Now

We may also be coloured by our previous negative life experiences, leaving us wounded and scared and affecting the way that we think and feel. This often leads us to live in the past or in the future, rather than in the present, because these options can seem so much more enticing to us than our present situation.

We may allow our negative past experiences to colour who we are and what we do in the present.

Perhaps we are also forever feeling anxious about what comes next.

I invite you to begin to think about this concept of time in a different way, which may help to put melancholy reminiscence or future catastrophising into context:

> *TTR: There is no past or future. There is only the eternal now.*

Trauma survivors in particular have a peculiar relationship with time. This is because people who have experienced trauma are experts at living where their trauma took place, rather than where they actually are, in the present moment.

We relive the horrible experience over and over again in our body-mind complex even though we might actually be sitting on the sofa in perfect safety.

Until we learn to be truly present, through feeling our bodies and reconnecting with our untraumatised Inner Self in *this* moment, we will still be subject to the fight-flight-freeze-flop response and all the negative body-mind symptoms living in this state creates.

This is why yoga can be so useful to us; it teaches us to feel our body and to meet it where it is today, in the present moment, regardless of what happened to us in the past or what might happen in the future.

Lao Tzu succinctly summarised the link between time and the emotional state in his well-known saying:

> TTR: "If you are depressed, you are living in the past.
>
> If you are anxious, you are living in the future.
>
> If you are at peace, you are living in the present."

Karma

Our past actions, good and bad, influence our current perceptions and actions and can distract us from knowing our Atma.

In yoga philosophy we call this Karma.

This does not mean that you are either a 'good' or a 'bad' person, but simply that for every action there is a consequence. There's no positive or negative value attributed to the action or the consequence, it is simply cause and effect: "You reap what you sow."

So, it's not:

> If you're really bad and steal all of your friends' stuff you'll go to Hell.

It's more:

If you steal all of your friends' stuff they won't like you and then you'll have no friends (unless they don't know that it was you, in which case you are a sneaky ninja, but please stop, because it's mean).

See, cause and effect:

Cause: stolen stuff.

Effect: Billy no-mates.

Sometimes we can't always perceive the potential karmic effects of what we do, but a good rule of thumb is to try to act with kindness, compassion and authenticity in all things. This way we are less likely to create Karma for ourselves that will have negative repercussions and unwelcome outcomes that we did not foresee.

The Koshas

Now we are coming back to the Koshas.

Earlier we looked at how the Koshas hide our Atma, our True Self, by creating the illusion of *maya*.

The best way to think of the Koshas is as a kind of *matryoshka* (Russian) doll, with our Atma being the last tiny little doll in the middle of the stack. When you initially pick the big doll up, you may believe that's all there is to the object, but when you start delving deeper, you realise that there are many other layers.

So it is with the Koshas.

We need to work with each of the layers, recognising and bypassing them until we reach the Atma inside and come to realise our True Nature.

In this way we are able to see through *maya* and recognise that we are already whole and perfect, in this present moment. When we do this, we no longer need to seek for happiness without, for we will have already found it within.

Below is another list of the Koshas and an explanation about what each of them is related to. We had a quick look earlier when we made our table, but here's a bit more detail:

1. Anna Maya Kosha: this is the physical body. 'Anna' literally means the 'food body' and refers to our muscles, joints, flesh, bones, blood and vital organs – all the tangible materials that make up our body. It can be seen, touched and felt. This is what we commonly think of as 'me'. The human-body-machine, the flesh suit in which we live for however many years we are alive on this magnificent planet. Anna Maya Kosha isn't the entirety of our being though, not by any stretch of the imagination.

A good way to begin investigating this concept is to ask yourself what happens to 'you' when you are asleep. When the physical body is no longer awake do 'you' disappear?

2. <u>Prana Maya Kosha:</u> this is the energy body. Prana is the universal life force that infuses all creation and our subtle anatomy. Prana is directed through energy centres in our bodies, known as Chakras, via channels known as nadis. *In yoga, special breathing techniques (*pranayama*) are used in order to strengthen, control or redirect the prana. The Prana Maya Kosha is essential to life on this plane, but, as ancient yogis were aspiring to a disembodied life beyond this plane, getting rid of this sheath didn't really bother them.*

3. <u>Mano Maya Kosha:</u> this refers to the mind body. 'Manas' means 'mind' in Sanskrit. This Kosha is composed of thoughts, concepts, beliefs and emotions. It's all the gumpf that goes back and forth in the space between your ears all day long. Mano Maya Kosha is one of the most difficult sheaths to shed, because so many of us are trapped in the misguided belief that our thoughts represent reality.

4. <u>Vijnana Maya Kosha:</u> this is the intuitive body or the imagination body. Vijnana is our *intuitive sense or direct awareness that spontaneously arises. Vijnana Maya Kosha is associated with mental clarity, intuition and the ability to become the impartial Witness.*

5. Ananda Maya Kosha: this is the bliss body, our most subtle layer. 'Ananda' translates as 'joy' or 'bliss' and consists of our innate qualities including inner peace, joy, wholeness and contentment. These are the qualities of our True Nature or our Inner Self and are independent of all possessions and external conditions.

Ida, Pingala and Sushumna

Prana was mentioned briefly in the previous section about the Koshas.

Prana is said to flow all over the human body in many channels, known as *nadis* (like little rivers through your tissue). In Yin Yoga, these *nadis* are roughly equivalent to the Chinese Meridian lines, which contain Chi (the same kind of thing as *prana*).

As you read earlier, yogis believe that trauma is an energy event, so an event which affects our *prana* or Chi. We can unblock our *nadis* (Meridian lines) through practising yoga and so avoid the sludgetastrophe that I was describing earlier.

Although there are lots and lots of *nadis* (Meridian lines), yogis believe that there are three major ones in the human body; two major energy currents that criss-cross one another on the left and right sides and a third that runs along the spine as a central channel.

You can imagine these channels as being like the two snakes that wrap around the caduceus on hospital symbols (ask the internet for a picture if you're not sure what I mean).

These channels are known as Ida, Pingala and Sushumna. They criss-cross backwards and forwards across the body, passing through the Chakras (see below) as they go. I haven't included a diagram, because there's some dissent over where each of these *nadis* begins and ends and how, exactly they ascend the body.

However:

- Ida is related to the parasympathetic nervous system and is associated with relaxation and the left side of the body (feminine restorative energy, often represented with a red/pink triangle with its point facing downwards).

In Yin theory, Ida relates to the Chandra (Yin) energies of the moon.

- Pingala is related to the sympathetic nervous system and is associated with tension and the

right side of the body (masculine, active energy, often represented by a blue triangle with its point facing upwards).

In Yin theory, Pingala relates to the Surya (Yang) energies of the sun.

-Sushumna can only be opened once Ida and Pingala are in balance. When Sushumna opens, energy, as a unified Spirit-force (kundalini), begins to rise and invert back to the Source/ Atman, merging at the Crown Chakra (Sahasrara Chakra).

In Yin theory, the Sushumna relates to the Governor Vessel.

When Ida and Pingala are in balance and Sushumna opens, it's possible to become aware of one's True Nature and to be in optimal health.

The Ida and Pingala *nadis* are related to the nostrils and the two halves of the brain.

The right nostril relates to the sympathetic nervous system (connecting with the left brain) and the left nostril relates to the parasympathetic nervous system (connecting with the right brain).

Usually we switch between right and left nostril dominance every 75 to 90 minutes, indicating a shift from left to right brain.

When you breathe equally through both nostrils, both halves of the brain are operating in unity and you feel balanced and full of equanimity (also energy is flowing through Sushumna).

But, if we are traumatised, we tend to spend more time with the sympathetic nervous system activated, which means that we breathe through our right nostril (rather than the left or an equal balance between the two).

I invite you now to investigate this for yourself, by trying the following exercise:

Exercise:

Place the palm of your hand under your nose, close your eyes if it feels comfortable for you to do so and breathe normally.

Which nostril is dominant?

Does this accurately represent your current state of mind?

Are you feeling calm or in touch with your emotions (left side)?

Are you feeling active, stressed or engaged (right side)?

Or are you perfectly at ease (both nostrils equally dominant)?

If you are feeling stressed throughout the day, this is a good little practice to undertake in order to check in with yourself and work out exactly what's going on.

Later in the book I will give you a practice called Alternate Nostril Breathing, which will help you to bring both of the brain hemispheres (and so your emotions and nervous system) back into equilibrium.

The Chakras

Yogis believe that Chakras (meaning 'wheel' or 'disc') act as energy transformers within the body.

They are located in the centre of the body, running roughly in line with the spine, but just in front of it.

Chakras transmute the universal energy of *prana* (or Chi), from air, light, water, thought, the environment and food, into biological energy to feed, sustain and nourish the organs and systems of the body.

They also manage the Spirit energy of the body, aiding the Spirit-force's journey through Sushumna and back to Source/ Atman.

When all the Chakras are open and unblocked, *kundalini* is able to rise and you are able to reach Enlightenment (if that's your goal).

I, personally, believe that Chakras are a metaphor for problems that we experience in our lives and that we have to work through the problems (unblock the Chakras) in order to feel happy and content (Enlightened).

Either way, here is a list of the Chakras and what they do:

> - *Muladhara:* your 'anchor', keeping you grounded physically and emotionally. The energy contained within this Chakra relates to basic survival needs (food, sleep etc.). If there is imbalance here you may be avoiding things that you need to address or you may start to develop fears.
>
> You mostly live in this Chakra when you are in a state of trauma. Hip openers are your friends; they help you to release any blockages here.
>
> - *Svadisthana:* related to your reproductive organs. The energy contained within this Chakra relates to your desires, the ability to soothe yourself and to be open to sensual pleasure. If there is imbalance here you may begin to develop attachments that are difficult to dislodge and that interrupt your life.

This Chakra may well become blocked if you have experienced sexual violence, for obvious reasons. Hip openers, although they can be triggering, are the way to balance this Chakra out again.

- Manipura: your 'power centre'. The energy contained within this Chakra relates to your purpose in the outside world. When this Chakra is clear you're able to carry out your individual purpose, whatever it might be. If there's imbalance here you may suffer from digestive issues and those related to metabolism. You may also express aggressive ambition and selfishness in your pursuits.

Do you get an upset stomach when you're stressed? It could be a blockage in your Manipura (doctors would call it stress-induced IBS). Twists are good for balancing this Chakra.

- Anahata: the seat of your ability to love, be compassionate and have faith. The energy contained within this Chakra relates to the lungs and the element of air, it's the central channel for the flow of your emotional experiences. If there's imbalance here you may radiate insecurity, despair and loneliness instead of love.

After experiencing trauma we tend to shut down and distance ourselves from others. This is a sign that Anahata is blocked. Backbends are helpful for opening us to loving experiences and unblocking this Chakra.

- Vishuddhi/ Visuddha: governs your speech and hearing. The energy contained within this Chakra relates to the endocrine glands and your ability to communicate your truths and to receive the truths of others, as well as converse freely and honestly. If there's imbalance here you may be avoiding speaking your truth or be resistant to hearing the truths of others.

Pretty much every person that I've met who has experienced trauma has a major issue with Vishuddhi. There's so much fear and shame around talking about your experiences and your feelings that it can take quite a while to release any blockages here. Throat opening asanas (e.g. backbends where the head drops back) are helpful for balancing this Chakra.

- Ajna: your 'Third Eye', is connected to both your physical and emotional growth. The energy contained within this Chakra allows your consciousness to flow freely through it and enables you to feel in touch with your intuition. It is related to the pituitary gland. If

there's an imbalance or a blockage here you may be ignoring the guidance of your intuition.

*This Chakra relates to PTG, about trusting yourself and becoming more self-aware. Breathing practices (*pranayama*) can be helpful for balancing this Chakra, because they help to turn the Stress Response off and calm you down, so that you can actually listen to and believe in yourself.*

- <u>Sahasrara:</u> the 'crown' of the Chakra system. The energy contained in this Chakra governs your highest state of development and enlightenment and is the gateway to everything beyond our normal range of experience. Thought is the expression of this Chakra. An overactive crown Chakra causes you to feel as though you are part of a spiritual elite and an underactive crown Chakra distances you from your own spirituality, causing scepticism and blocking you from spiritual development.

So, when you're having racing or negative thoughts, you might have an issue with your Crown. If you believe that you are the only Enlightened one on this planet and that you alone know the way to Everlasting Happiness, you probably also have something going on up there.

This Chakra also relates to the spiritual development aspect of PTG. When you have no blockages, you may begin to see the world in a different way and become more connected to your underlying Atma. Meditation is the best way to balance this Chakra. Yin Yoga and Yoga Nidra are both meditation-inducing practices.

The Chakras, the *nadis* and the Koshas form the basis of energy theory within yoga practice. The information I've provided in this chapter should, hopefully, help you to understand why yogic practices can be helpful with alleviating the energetic blockage caused by experiencing trauma.

There is, of course, lots more to yoga, but I'm not going to go into its history and development here, because it's a vast subject and beyond the scope of this book. However, the resources listed in the bibliography will provide you with lots more information on the subject, if you are interested to learn more.

CHAPTER THIRTEEN

PRECAUTIONS AND ADVICE FOR PRACTICE

First of all, please observe the disclaimer at the beginning of this book and make sure that you seek appropriate advice from qualified medical professionals about whether or not the following practices are suitable for you.

I am *not* a medical professional.

Nor do I know your own particular set of circumstances and how appropriate it might be for you to do some or all of the practices described in this book.

The Relaxation Response

In all of the yogic practices described in this book, we are trying to induce the Relaxation Response. Whilst usually helpful and deeply healing, the Relaxation

Response can also occasionally cause unwanted physical, mental and emotional effects in some people.

These effects can range from feeling dissociated from your body or reality, to sudden anxiety, irritation or panic. It's also possible that deeply repressed emotions will surface (see more on this below).

You may experience a drop in blood pressure or a temporary hypoglycemic state as a result of relaxation practices (see precautions listed for Shavasana, which also apply to the practice of Yoga Nidra, as it is usually carried out in this shape).

I advise that the first time you practise any of the techniques found here you advise a friend, partner or relative of your intention and consult any doctors/ mental health professionals that you are seeing regularly prior to beginning your practice.

It's rare that you'll experience serious side-effects from eliciting the Relaxation Response and, indeed, some of them can be helpful for your continued emotional and spiritual growth (e.g. working through and releasing the deep emotional blockages that your trauma has caused). Below I include some advice about sitting with these disturbances to get the most out of your practice, but your own tolerance level must always be your guide, as everybody reacts differently.

If in doubt, always seek appropriate assistance.

Disturbances

You may be disturbed in several ways when practising yoga. These disturbances can include, but aren't limited to:

> - *Somebody disturbing you.*
>
> - *A phone ringing or some other intrusive noise.*
>
> - *Thoughts that arise during the practice.*
>
> - *Strong emotions that arise during the practice.*
>
> - *Uncomfortable bodily sensations that arise during the practice.*

In all cases it will be possible to return to the practice following the disturbance.

If it's a physical interruption, then calmly return to the practice once you have spoken to the person, turned off your phone etc. It is, obviously, best to remember to turn off (or at least put on 'silent') the phone or any other devices before practice, so that these interruptions don't occur.

If your body is uncomfortable, you have the option to stay with the sensations and try to habituate yourself to them or you can alter position if it is really painful.

> *TTR: Choices Are Endless (CAE). You can always choose another form, skip an* asana *that you don't like or use props to assist. You can also come out of a form or Nidra whenever you like.*

If thoughts and emotions disturb you, this is an indicator that the yoga practice is having an effect for you.

Day-to-day thoughts (what am I going to have for dinner? etc.) may be dismissed.

Simply acknowledge the thought and then let it pass you by, like a cloud on a sunny day.

If the thought or emotion is incredibly disturbing for you, you must decide whether to 'sit' with it or to come out of the practice and inform your instructor (if practising in a 'live' environment).

If you're alone you should come out of the form or Nidra and inform a trusted friend or medical/ mental health professional as soon as practicably possible, if you feel particularly distressed by what you were thinking or experiencing.

Possible Adverse Effects

There's a high chance that you will feel some periods of disturbance or distress and you are the one who decides whether or not this is tolerable to you. You may find that your tolerance for the disturbances increases, as you work through your trauma and experience PTG. You may also find that your tolerance varies from day-to-day, depending on what else is going on in your life at the time.

As you've likely realised by now, we tend to repress unpleasant thoughts and emotions that arise as a result of our life experiences and, because of this, those thoughts, emotions and resultant physical sensations get 'stuck'.

Remember that sludgeberg from earlier.

Practising yoga loosens and removes the energetic blockages that have prevented these thoughts, emotions and physical sensations from being expressed and integrated into the body-mind complex and so you will experience them re-emerging at some point during your practice.

This is a good thing, as long as the experience doesn't frighten you. If it does, then you need to end the practice immediately and consult a medical/ mental health professional as soon as practicably possible.

You must be your own guide in this.

You have to trust in the innate healing wisdom of your soul.

While it's true that growth and healing occur when we work through our most difficult thoughts, feelings and emotions, everybody's tolerance level is different.

Don't push yourself further than you feel comfortable with and understand that your tolerance levels (both in terms of physical and emotional/ psychological discomfort) will vary from day-to-day and from practice to practice.

Whether you decide to sit with these experiences, or not, just decide to be kind to yourself.

TTR: You can develop your interoceptive skills by respecting where your body-mind complex is today and meeting it where it is, rather than where you would like it to be.

Physical Precautions

When practising the *asanas* listed in the next chapter, ensure that you observe and react to any sensations of sharp pain, tingling and numbness. If any of these sensations are present come out of the form immediately, as they are indicative of an impending injury or a potential nerve compression.

Pregnancy: If you're pregnant, you must take extra care when practising Yin Yoga, due to the presence of the hormone relaxin. This means that your joints will already be looser than normal and you'll have a greater range of movement. Going too deep into a shape could cause injury. Always seek your doctor's or consultant's advice before beginning a physical yoga practice and carefully observe the contraindications and modifications described for each form.

Hypermobility: If you're hypermobile you must take extra care during a Yin Yoga practice, as it's very easy to hyperextend a joint and cause yourself pain or injury. Instead of totally relaxing the muscles during practice, you may find it helpful to engage them (e.g. the tops of the thighs during Dragonfly) to stabilise your joints. I also strongly advocate the use of props however and wherever you need them. This is your practice and there's no shame at all in using props to protect your body, if you feel comfortable doing so.

Triggers: Please remember that some of the forms described may be triggering for you if you are suffering from the symptoms of PTS or PTSD/ PTSI. As we are all unique and our traumas not the same, it's difficult for me to identify precisely which forms each individual will find triggering. However, I can advise caution generally with forms that expose vulnerable parts of your body (e.g. Reclining Dragon may be especially triggering to survivors of sexual assault) or remind you of previous training if you are a military veteran (e.g. the Dragons strongly resemble 'taking a knee'). You may also find the use of some props to be uncomfortable, depending on the nature of the traumatic event that you experienced (e.g. belts or straps can be triggering to those who have had their movements restricted), so please consider this when choosing whether or not to use them in your practice.

TTR: You should use your own intuition and feelings when deciding which forms and props you might find beneficial and which you will likely find triggering.

Sequencing: Whilst I have suggested some possible sequences for the forms, please don't feel that you have to adhere to these. I invite you to modify them as appropriate for your body and situation. A good principle to remember, when constructing your own sequences, is to consider the motion that your body is going through. As a general rule, it's good to add forward bends to counteract backbends and twists to ensure that your body has been taken through all planes of movement. However you decide to structure your practice, please do heed the advice above and listen to what your body needs on any given day. If my back is causing me a lot of pain, for example, I might choose to avoid any forward folds, as these can aggravate lower back injury.

Counter-forms: Remember that, although they are described, counter-forms in Yin Yoga are advised rather than essential. It's good practice, though, to work the body evenly on both sides and for the same period of time, unless pain or injury prevents you from doing so.

> *TTR: The* asanas *are described with contraindications and modifications suitable for generally healthy individuals. Yin is NOT Restorative yoga and you should expect to feel sensations (not all of them pleasant) during your practice.*

Illness and medication: If you're taking particular medications, have identified illnesses (especially cardiac problems or diabetes), injuries or are simply unsure whether or not this practice is suitable for you, you should always consult a medical and/ or mental health professional before beginning your practice. If in doubt about how to perform any of the yogic techniques listed, please do seek the advice of a reputable yoga teacher for guidance in a 'live' environment (some websites that you might find helpful are listed in the bibliography).

CHAPTER FOURTEEN

TRAUMA INFORMED YIN YOGA (TIYY)

In this chapter I'm going to share with you what I like to think of as Trauma Informed Yin Yoga (TIYY):

> - _Trauma informed_; because we are considering the effects that each shape might have on our body-mind complex and only choosing those that feel good or beneficial to us, with awareness of what we might find triggering or upsetting according to our own circumstances.
>
> - _'Yin Yoga'_; because this is a slightly different practice to the more active 'Yang' styles of yoga that you might be more familiar with.

My TIYY practice might be very different from what yours turns out to be, but, to give you a base-line to start from, I've described the forms that I use (including how to get into them and come out of them safely) and how I feel that each shape benefits me.

You may have a very different experience with the forms and I invite you to explore and to experiment with the shapes, so that you can create a practice that feels good to you.

What is Yin Yoga?

Yin Yoga is derived from 'traditional' yoga, but can be viewed as a kind of evolution of the ancient practice.

Unlike traditional yoga practices, Yin Yoga incorporates Chinese meridian theory within its philosophy and works on the deeper connective tissues of the body (the fascia) rather than the muscles (as in Yang styles).

Many people perceive Yin Yoga to be a way of accessing a greater range of movement, through lengthening and strengthening the ligaments and tendons, but it's also a good way to meet your 'edge' and to foster a more meditative attitude.

TTR: You 'edge' can be either mental or physical. It's the point that, if you go beyond it, you will incur physical, mental or emotional injury. Finding your edge can take some practise and I encourage you to go gently and cautiously towards it, rather than rushing and hurting yourself.

Your edge will be different on different days.

Long hold times encourage the practitioner to stay with any uncomfortable sensations and to understand that in their discomfort it's possible to find growth. This is achieved through developing your ability to interocept (understand and feel what's going on inside your body).

This is why Yin Yoga is particularly helpful to trauma survivors like us, because our interoceptive skills are generally not as finely tuned as those of an untraumatised person.

TTR: Interoception is the ability to feel what is going on within the body-mind complex (for example, a dry throat indicating thirst or the ability to feel ourselves breathing or sensing when our muscles are tense). This ability allows us to develop a reliable sense of 'self' that makes us feel safe within our own body and, consequently, within the world around us.

Yin Yoga encourages the practitioner to become somatically present, by learning to pay attention to the minute sensations within their body, in the quiet that arises without movement, sound and active thought processes.

Again, I'm not going to go into any great detail about the history of the practice, but the main figures in the development of Yin Yoga are; Paulie Zink, Paul Grilley, Sarah Powers, Bernie Clark, Biff Mithoefer and Norman Blair.

I thoroughly recommend you reading any (or all) of their books, which go into lots of detail about how Yin Yoga was born from a Taoist interpretation of yoga practice, as well as giving plenty of ideas for sequencing and modifying the *asanas*.

Some of their various works are listed in the bibliography.

A Bit About The *Asanas*

I'm going to tell you which *asanas* work for me and suggest a couple of sequences that you might like to try.

There are more Yin *asanas* than I've listed and explained here, but these are the ones that I use regularly. Some of them go by different names, depending on the teacher. Some teachers use more, some less. I personally use all of the forms listed at some point in my Yin Yoga week, but I have some that I like more than others.

Some I haven't included simply because I don't practise them that often.

With practise, you'll get to know which of these you prefer and which you like less:

1. Ankle Stretch
2. Butterfly
3. Constructive Rest
4. Deer
5. Dragonfly
6. Eye of the Needle
7. Reclining Dragon
8. Reclining Twist
9. Resting on Heels
10. Saddle
11. Shavasana (Resting Form)
12. Sphinx and Seal
13. Squat
14. Upper Body Shapes
15. Yin Inversion

Hopefully this list should be enough to pique your interest and from it you might go on to discover even more Yin shapes or, alternatively, you might decide that these forms are more than enough.

Introspection vs. Expansion

Before I explain how to get into the forms, I just briefly want to explain the rationale behind the shapes that I've chosen.

Yin Yoga is traditionally thought of as a forward folding, introspective practice. In my personal experience, trauma survivors have generally introspected more than we probably should've done already and, actually, we need to begin reconnecting with both our bodies and the world around us, rather than going any further down the rabbit-holes within our own minds. Most days I really don't benefit from getting any more into my own head than I already am, so my practice is based upon grounding and opening.

This is why I prefer shapes that make me feel strong (like Squat) and spacious (like a backbend in Saddle).

My aim is to always expand my energy outwards and to feel connected to the world around me, rather than directing my energy inwards and withdrawing from a world that I already feel a little separate and dissociated from.

Also, as I mentioned earlier, backbends and upright shapes activate your sternocleidomastoid muscle (the curiousity muscle). So, I don't want my head to slump downwards on my neck in a forward bend, I want it to be up and alert in a shape such as Sphinx or open and supported by the ground as I recline in Butterfly.

This doesn't mean that I'm not relaxing (supported backbends feel absolutely wonderful to me), but it does mean that I'm not falling into the trap of sinking back inside myself and ruminating over everything that has gone wrong in my life or catastrophising over all the things that I still fear.

Hopefully, this will work as well for you as it does for me and I invite you to explore feeling open and spacious, curious and expansive.

Controversial, perhaps, but, for me, Yin is mostly about backbends.

Sara's 5 Principles of TIYY

There are 5 principles that I invite you to follow (as well as observing the precautions and advice of the previous chapter) when practising Yin Yoga:

1. Come to an appropriate edge: this is the place where you feel physical and mental sensation (not pain, but you should feel something).

2. Be still: try not to itch your nose, fidget, pick at your nail varnish, but do move if you are in pain. Tingling sensations, electrical sensations and 'oh God my patella just dislocated' are appropriate times to readjust or leave a shape.

3. Remain for a period of time: how long is up to you; three to five minutes is fine, but you may want to just do a minute when you first start.

4. Come out of the form with care: because you've been stretching your connective tissues for a while and you don't want to damage them by moving them too quickly.

5.Respect where your body and mind are today: just because you could get into a form yesterday, doesn't necessarily mean that you will be able to do so again today. Some days you may be able to stay for five minutes, on other days a minute is more than enough.

TTR: Everyone's pain threshold is different and yours will be different on different days, so always listen to and respect your body where it is today. Please be kind to yourself.

The Practicalities of Practice

You can do the practice in silence or you can listen to music.

You don't need a mat, although you may be more comfortable practising on one (or a folded blanket). Yin yoga is accessible to you wherever you are.

You can use props if you want to, but these don't have to be fancy. Pillows and cushions work well instead of bolsters and big fat books can be used as blocks.

Some days you might want to use props, other days you might be happy just to let your body do the work.

You might find props triggering, in which case don't try to introduce them into your practice until you feel ready to or maybe not at all.

> *TTR: Props are there to improve your practice. If you find them triggering or unhelpful, you don't have to use them.*

As to how often you practice, the choice, as ever, is yours.

I practice every day, but you will soon figure out how often feels good for you.

As a general rule:

> *TTR: If in doubt, it's better to do little and often, rather than a lot only occasionally, which we can apply to Yoga Nidra as well as to Yin.*

1. Ankle Stretch

I like to use this form as a preparation for Saddle, holding for perhaps a minute, before reclining back. However, sometimes it's nice simply to pause here and welcome in sensation. With the head held high, chin level and sternocleidomastoid muscle engaged, I find that Ankle Stretch is a good place from which to ponder the comings and goings of the world.

Benefits:

- Opens and strengthens the ankles.
- Can be used as a preparatory shape or counter-form.

Contraindications:

- Any sharp pain in the ankles means that you need to ease off or stop.
- Be aware of any tingling sensations in the feet; this could mean that you are compressing a nerve and need to ease off or stop.
- Any knee issues.
- Any ankle ankles.
- You can try using cushions or rolled blankets under the ankles, behind the knees or between the calves to help.

How to get into the form:

- Come into a kneeling position and sit back onto your heels.

Modifications:

- Lean back on your hands initially, keeping the heart open and maybe a slight backbend.
- When you feel comfortable, bring your hands either onto your knees or onto the floor beside you.
- You may rock back even further on your heels and pull the knees gently towards you or you may bring the hands back into Reverse Prayer form.
- If your ankles or knees sharply complain at any point, come out of the form.

How to come out of the form:

- Lean forward, so that the weight is off of your heels.
- Use the hands to take your weight, as you roll onto the outer thigh and swing the legs forwards.

Counter-forms:

- Squat.

- Any positon that tucks the toes under and straightens the legs (counter-flexion of the ankles).

2. Butterfly

Butterfly is a versatile form that can be used as a backbending or forward-folding shape. For me, because I see Yin Yoga as a practice of expansion rather than introversion, I like to bend backwards and open my heart to the world and the universe, welcoming sensations in at the same time as sending my presence outwards. It's a beautiful meditative shape, as well as an effective hip-opener.

Benefits:

- Stretches the lower back.
- Hamstring stretch (if the feet are further from the body).
- Adductor stretch (if the feet are closer to the body).
- Can be performed as a forward fold or a backbend.

Contraindications:

- Sciatica or lower back issues.
- Neck issues.
- You could sit on a block or cushion to bring the knees lower than the hips to help with any back complaint.
- You could keep the spine straight, rather than rounding it and folding forward.

- You could bend backwards, which can be a relief for some lower back issues.
- Avoid this form all together if it aggravates pain.

How to get into the form:

- From sitting, bring the soles of the feet together and then slide them forwards.
- You should have roughly two hand lengths between your heels and your body.

Modifications:

- Stay upright, with the heart open and hands resting on your knees or by your sides.
- Fold backwards, perhaps placing a cushion or yoga bolster (length-ways) beneath your spine to accentuate the backbend or give support. Feel free to play around with levels of support or simply fold back to the floor.
- You can fold forward, holding the feet and allowing the head to drop. I generally don't recommend this until you feel more comfortable with the practice, as it is a very introspective position. Be guided in this by your own thoughts and feelings on each given day.

- You may want to place blocks or cushions under your knees for extra support, if your knees are some distance from the ground.
- You may want to sit on a block or cushion to elevate your hips above your knees, if folding forwards.

How to come out of the form:

- Lean back on your hands to take the weight off the legs, if upright or folded forwards, then slowly and carefully straighten the legs.
- If folded backwards, simply straighten the legs to Shavasana and then roll onto your side before coming up to a seated position.

Counter-forms:

- If you folded forward, lean back on the hands and counter-form with a gentle backbend.
- If you folded backwards, you can come into Resting on Heels.

3. Constructive Rest

The pause in the beat that is your practice of Yin. Constructive Rest is a great shape to use between other *asanas*, a way to give your body and mind a break from the sensations and emotions that can arise within practice. It's also a nice alternative to Shavasana that you can use to close the practice, if you so wish.

Benefits:

- Relaxes the iliopsoas muscle (connecting spine, pelvis and femur).
- Can be a generally relaxing and restoring form.
- A good form to begin/ end a practice with.
- A good resting form.

Contraindications:

- If pregnant (particularly after week 16) should avoid this form or seek a medical professional's advice before performing.
- If you have low blood pressure or a heart condition, come up out of the form very slowly and seek a medical professional's advice before performing.
- If remaining in this position for some time, blood pressure can drop and a temporary

hypoglycemic state can occur (due to deep relaxation).

- Caution is advised for people taking insulin, sedatives or cardiovascular medications.
- The Relaxation Response triggered by this shape can have some adverse effects, including, but not limited to; anxiety, dissociation and powerful emotional response.
- Read the earlier general precaution about the Relaxation Response.

How to get into the form:

- Begin lying on your back.
- Bend your knees and bring the soles of the feet up to touch the floor.
- Keep your feet flat on the floor, hip width apart.
- Allow the knees to drop inwards until they touch.
- Arms can rest by your sides or above your head.

Modifications:

- You may wish to experiment with the position of the feet; taking them wider or closer together.

- You may want to bring the heels closer to the hips or take them further away.
- You may want to use a strap or belt to hold the knees together and take some of the effort out of the form.
- You can place a cushion between your knees or under your lower back.
- You can recline onto a cushion or bolster, placed length-ways along the spine.
- You can experiment with the position of the arms and hands.

How to come out of the form:

- Loosen the belt or strap (if used).
- Extend the legs along the ground.
- Use the hands to slowly assist you into a sitting position.
- Roll onto the right side (the left if you are pregnant or have low blood pressure) and use the hands to help you to slowly come up to sitting.
- Always come out of the form slowly and cautiously, especially if you have been lying still for a long time.

Counter-forms:

- None required.

- Constructive Rest may be used as a resting form between other shapes or as a form for Yoga Nidra/ meditation.

4. Deer

For me, this is a restful shape. In Deer I invoke the spirit of the animal for which it's named; quiet, peaceful and observant. I keep my chin up and the sternocleidomastoid muscle engaged, maintaining my curiousity about the world even as my hips settle and my sit-bones root down.

Benefits:

- Can be used as a counter-form to hip openers or any external rotation of the hips.
- Rotates the hips internally (back leg) and externally (front leg).
- Can be combined with Upper Body Shapes.

Contraindications:

- Knee issues; take care when externally rotating the hip (front knee) by keeping that foot closer to the groin.
- You can support the knees with a folded blanket if they are particularly sensitive.
- Some people may be sensitive in their knees and iliotibial band when performing internal rotation (back leg), so be mindful of any sharp pains or tingling sensations in the back leg.

How to get into the form:

- Start by sitting in Butterfly.
- Swing one leg behind you, bringing the foot behind your hip.
- Move the foot of the front leg away from you, making a right angle with the front knee if you can.
- Move the back foot away from the hip, until you feel a tipping away from that foot.
- Make sure your sitting bones are pressing firmly into the ground and that you feel stable.

Modifications:

- You could combine this form with any of the Upper Body Shapes.
- You may want to experiment with the position of your front foot.
- You may want to experiment with the position of the back foot.

How to come out of the form:

- Take the weight off of the back foot, by leaning away from it.
- Swing the back foot forwards and come back into Butterfly.
- Change to the other side.

<u>Counter-forms:</u>

- Do the other side.

5. Dragonfly

I enjoy performing Dragonfly as the opening shape to my morning routine. Initially I hated the stretch that it gave to my inner thighs and lower back and I tried to avoid it wherever possible, but when I finally stopped fighting the form and allowed my body to soften, I found that it was actually one of the most soothing *asanas*. It really is true that the shape you avoid the most is often the one that you need the most.

Benefits:

- Opens the hips.
- Opens the groin.
- Opens the backs of the thighs.
- Opens the inner knees.

Contraindications:

- If you are pregnant then avoid the wall version of this shape and don't fold too far forwards, so that the belly is not compressed.
- Can aggravate lower back issues and sciatica. Sit on a block or cushion to elevate the hips above the knees to ease this.
- Can aggravate knee issues, so engage the quadriceps or place support beneath the knees to create a curve (be especially careful about this if you are hypermobile).

- This posture could be triggering for some, as it exposes vulnerable areas of your body. Proceed with caution.

How to get into the form:

- From a sitting position, extend the legs wide.
- Allow the feet to relax.
- Remain upright or gently begin to fold forwards.

Modifications:

- If folding forwards, you can place a bolster on its end and rest the forehead against it.
- You can perform this lying on your back, with you buttocks shuffled up against a wall, using the wall to support your legs.
- If you perform this shape against the wall, either take hold of the thighs and draw them slightly towards you, so that there is a slight bend in the knees and they don't fall too far outwards, or place blocks under each thigh to control the effect of gravity.

How to come out of the form:

- If you folded forwards, use the hands to push away from the floor and slowly come up.

- Use the hands to gently draw the legs together and lean back on your hands to create a slight back bend.

- Gently shake out the legs and feet.

- If performing against the wall, use the hands to draw the legs together and then slowly roll onto your side (left if you are pregnant or have low blood pressure), before coming up to a sitting form and shaking the legs and feet out.

Counter-forms:

- Windshield Wipers can be a nice counter-form, gently turning the knees from side to side.

6. Eye of the Needle

For me this shape is sort of like giving my body a little hug at the same time as gently opening the hips. It can be a nice shape to try at the end of a busy day or when the world is getting a little on top of you. I simply lie back and let Mother Earth support me, as I draw my legs in close.

Benefits:

- Opens the hips, by abducting the thigh of the bent leg.
- Activates the gluteal muscles, the buttocks and the quadriceps.

Contraindications:

- Avoid if pregnant (especially past week 16) or seek a medical professional's advice before performing.
- Avoid if you have a heart condition/ blood pressure issues which mean that you shouldn't remain horizontal for a prolonged period or seek a medical professional's advice before performing and take particular care in coming up out of the shape to avoid dizziness and fainting.

- Knee issues; external rotation can aggravate existing knee injuries or weaknesses, similarly for iliotibial band injuries.

How to get into the form:

- Begin lying on your back.
- Bend the knees and place the soles of the feet on the floor.
- Cross one ankle across the opposite knee.
- You can stay here, with the arms falling away from you, or you can thread one arm between the legs and the other round the outside of the supporting leg and hug the knee into the chest.

Modifications:

- You can place cushions under the lower back, if your spine feels uncomfortable.
- You can place the supporting foot against a wall to take the strain of the shape and allow your hands to drop open by your sides.

How to come out of the form:

- Reverse the process of coming into the shape.
- Release the leg, if hugging into the chest, so that the foot of the supporting leg is once again flat against the floor.

- Uncross the ankle, so that the soles of both feet are flat on the floor.
- Change to the other side.

Counter-forms:

- Change to the other side.

7. Reclining Dragon

I used to find this form intensely uncomfortable, as it made me feel incredibly vulnerable. It can be triggering for survivors of sexual assault, for obvious reasons, but it is also a good way to reclaim your power. I now practise Reclining Dragon every single day and feel incredibly comfortable and capable when doing so. It reminds me that my body is mine and no one else's. It's a shape to build up to in your own space and time.

Benefits:

- A deep hip opener.
- Can be used either as the full form or as Half Reclining Dragon.
- Releases and decompresses the sacroiliac (SI) joints.

Contraindications:

- Avoid if pregnant (especially past week 16) or seek a medical professional's advice before performing.
- If the hips roll up off the floor this becomes a mild inversion, so do not perform if you have any heart conditions/ blood pressure issues that could make this dangerous for you (make

sure to seek a medical professional's advice before performing).

- If you have lower back disorders, which do not allow flexion of the spine, don't allow the hips to come up off of the floor.
- Women on their menstrual cycles may not wish to invert.
- If there are SI joint issues don't go too deep and consider using cushions to support under the lower back.
- This can be a triggering shape for those who have experienced sexual assault or any kind of sexual violence. If you feel at all vulnerable going into or performing this shape, then avoid it.

How to get into the form:

- Begin lying on your back and hug the knees into the chest.
- Take hold of the soles of the feet, the ankles or the backs of the legs.
- Open the feet apart, so that they are above your knees.
- Gently guide the knees towards the floor, by pulling on your feet.
- Relax the head and shoulders down to the floor.

Modifications:

- You can do one foot at a time, allowing the other leg to extend along the floor in Half Reclining Dragon.
- You can use a strap or belt to hold the feet and guide the knees down (this could be triggering for some).
- You can hold the backs of the thighs.
- You can do this with the soles of the feet pushing against the wall, like a lying down Squat.
- Don't pull too vigorously on the feet – relax and let gravity do the work as your body opens.

How to come out of the form:

- Release the feet and allow them to gently fall back to the floor, so that the soles of the feet are on the ground and the knees are bent.
- You can pause here for a moment or go into Constructive Rest.

Counter-forms:

- A gentle backbend, such as Sphinx.
- You can also drop the knees from side to side in a Windshield Wiper; sitting with weight supported on the hands or lying with your feet

flat on the floor and your knees bent, gently allow the legs to drop from side to side. This is an internal rotation to counteract the external rotation of Reclining Dragon.

- If performing Half Reclining Dragon, make sure that you change sides.

8. Reclining Twist

For me, this shape is quite simply, wonderful! There are so many options with this form; position of head, arms and legs. There are so many ways to experiment and it's a wonderful shape for stretching over-worked backs (particularly if you spend all day hunched over a desk). A word of caution though; many people find Reclining Twists so relaxing that they accidentally drop off to sleep!

Benefits:

- Rotates and stretches the spine.
- Relaxes the mind.
- Opens the chest and heart.
- Can be helpful for lower back issues.

Contraindications:

- Avoid if pregnant (especially past week 16) or seek a medical professional's advice before performing.
- Avoid if you have a heart condition/ blood pressure issues which mean that you shouldn't remain horizontal for a prolonged period or seek a medical professional's advice before performing and take particular care in

coming up out of the shape to avoid dizziness and fainting.

- Shoulder issues; injuries to the shoulder or if you are prone to tingling in the hands when you raise your arms over your head. You may want to keep both of the hands resting on the body.

How to get into the form:

- Begin lying on your back.
- Gently shift the hips the opposite way to which you intend to drop the knees, so if dropping the knees to the right, shift the hips only a few inches to the left.
- Hug the knees into the chest.
- Allow the knees to drop to one side, stacking the knees on top of one another.
- The hand on the side you are twisting towards rests on the knees, the other stretches out alongside your body in a 'T' shape. You can press the palm into the floor or allow it to face upwards, do whichever feels most comfortable for you.

Modifications:

- You may wish to place some support under the knees, if your knees don't reach the floor (e.g. a block, bolster or cushions).
- You may wish to place some support under the outstretched arm, if your shoulder is up off of the floor (e.g. cushions or a bolster).
- You may wish to experiment with the position of the knees; bringing them closer to the armpit intensifies the stretch.

How to come out of the form:

- Slowly roll onto your back.
- Hug the knees into the chest for a moment to release the sacrum and lumbar spine.

Counter-forms:

- Change sides.

9. Resting on Heels

Resting on Heels is both a gentle forward fold and a mild inversion. There's something very reminiscent of the womb in the sensation of being supported by the Earth and your own body. Resting on Heels is deeply nurturing, as well as a good counter-form to a practice that involves lots of active backbends. In Resting on Heels I find it easy to release and let go.

Benefits:

- A deeply restful and soothing form.
- Gentle stretch for the spine.
- Mild inversion.

Contraindications:

- Don't perform if pregnant.
- Don't perform if you have diarrhoea.
- Knee issues may be aggravated; use rolled blankets or cushions for support or avoid the form altogether.
- Ankle issues may be aggravated; use rolled blankets or cushions for support or avoid the form altogether.
- As this is a mild inversion, it may not be suitable for those with a heart condition or blood pressure issues (check with a medical professional before performing).

How to get into the form:

- Sit on the heels and then slowly fold forwards.
- Bring your chest towards your thighs and your forehead towards the floor.

Modifications:

- Arms may be outstretched in front of you (relaxes the shoulders and reduces the pressure on the neck).
- Arms may fold back behind you, taking the weight of the form onto your forehead.
- You can support the forehead on your hands or a block or bolster if your buttocks don't touch your heels (to reduce pressure on the neck and head).
- The heels and knees can be closer together or wider apart (feel free to experiment to find the most comfortable position for you).
- You can place a bolster length-ways under your chest and torso to make the form more restorative.

How to come out of the form:

- Push the floor away from you with your hands and slowly sit upright.

Counter-forms:

- None necessary.
- Resting on Heels can be used as a resting form whenever you feel the need to take a break, or as a counter-form to backbends.

10. Saddle

This can be a challenging shape for some, but it's one that I really enjoy. It shares some of the back-bending qualities of Sphinx/ Seal with the rejuvenating power of Shavasana. This is a go-to form for me, when I need to stretch and quieten in the middle of a hectic or particularly stressful day.

Benefits:

- Compresses the sacral-lumbar arch.
- Stretches the hip flexors and quadriceps.
- Opens the heart.
- Relaxes the mind if performed as a supported backbend.
- It can feel good for some people with lower back issues.

Contraindications:

- Avoid folding backwards if pregnant (especially past week 16) or seek a medical professional's advice before performing.
- Avoid folding backwards if you have a heart condition/ blood pressure issues which mean that you shouldn't remain horizontal for a prolonged period or seek a medical professional's advice before performing and

take particular care in coming up out of the shape to avoid dizziness and fainting.

- Back issues, including SI joint problems.
- Knee issues; be careful of the knees. This may be too intense a shape for some. Use caution if you have had previous knee injuries or iliotibial band injuries.
- Ankle issues; this can be too intense for some.
- If you feel any sharp or burning pain in this shape you must come out.
- Consider using a folded blanket under the knees/ ankles to offer support.
- Don't raise the arms overhead if there are any shoulder issues or injuries or if you experience tingling or numbness in the hands with the arms in this position.

How to get into the form:

- From a kneeling position, simply sit on the heels.
- If there is no pain in heels or ankle, lean back onto the hands and see how this feels.
- If there is still no pain, you can come further back onto the elbows or onto a bolster placed lengthways along the spine.

- If this feels ok, you can consider performing the shape without the bolster, coming all the way back so that you are flat on your back.
- The arms can then be raised overhead (if there are no shoulder issues) or allowed to fall open on either side of your body.

Modifications:

- You can place a block between the thighs, under the buttocks, and sit on that to relieve pressure on the knees and ankles.
- You can intensify the form by taking the feet out on either side of the buttocks and sitting between them (proceed with caution, as this is a very strong internal rotation).
- You can allow the knees to widen as you bend backwards, if this is more comfortable for your body.
- You can do one leg at a time, either keeping the opposite leg outstretched along the floor or hugging the knee into the chest (this is a very strong shape, so proceed with caution and listen to your body).
- If you do one leg at a time, make sure you do both sides of the body.

How to come out of the form:

- The easiest way to come out is to come back up the way you went in.
- Prop yourself up onto your elbows and hands, so that you are once more sitting on your heels.
- You can then come forwards onto the belly, straightening the legs and tucking the toes under.
- You could try rolling onto one side and slowly straightening each leg in turn.
- If you are very flexible, you may simply be able to untuck the feet.

Counter-forms:

- If you do one leg at a time, make sure you do both sides of the body.
- Whilst lying on your back, gently hug the knees into the chest to release the lower back.
- You can slowly and gently move into Resting on Heels Form.

11. Shavasana (Resting Form)

Shavasana provides me with an excuse to simply let go of the world around me. For five, ten, fifteen, sometimes twenty minutes I can be everywhere and nowhere all at the same time. I expand and contract simultaneously into a space of just being. For me, this shape is deeply relaxing and rejuvenating.

Benefits:

- Can be a deeply relaxing and healing form.
- Allows the entire body-mind complex to relax, especially when combined with breathing exercises or Yoga Nidra.
- Can be used during meditation.

Contraindications:

- Avoid if pregnant (especially past week 16) or seek a medical professional's advice before performing.
- Avoid if you have a heart condition/ blood pressure issues which mean that you shouldn't remain horizontal for a prolonged period or seek a medical professional's advice before performing and take particular care in coming up out of the shape to avoid dizziness and fainting.

- Be aware that remaining for long periods and triggering the Relaxation Response can have adverse effects in some people (see earlier advice).
- Blood pressure can drop if you remain for a long period.
- If you remain for a long period, you may temporarily become hypoglycemic.
- Always check with your health care professional before practising if you are on any medications, particularly insulin, sedatives or cardiovascular medications.

How to get into the form:

- Lay on you back.
- Your feet can be hip width apart and dropping open, so that neither the feet nor the thighs are touching.
- Your hands can rest by your sides, so that they aren't touching the body.
- Your eyes can be open or closed.
- If open, try to keep your gaze soft.

Modifications:

- You can try propping your heels up on cushions, so that the legs are elevated (snuggling the buttocks close to a sofa and putting the feet up is a good way to achieve this at home).

- You can place a bolster or cushions underneath your spine, lengthways.
- You can place low blocks or cushions under the hands, to give the elbows a slight bend.

How to come out of the form:

- Roll onto the right side and use the hands to push yourself up to a seated position.
- Roll onto the left side if pregnant or if you have low blood pressure.
- Take care coming upright, make sure that you move slowly and carefully, particularly if you have been resting in Shavasana for a prolonged period.

Counter-forms:

- None required.
- Shavasana is a good shape to both open and close a practice with.

12. Sphinx and Seal

These two shapes feel particularly wonderful to me. They are a time for reflection. I keep my head neutral in these forms, not allowing my head to drop, with the sternocleidomastoid muscle engaged. I feel grounded, present and supported.

Benefits:

- Compression and stimulation for the sacral-lumbar arch.
- Can be particularly therapeutic for those with herniated or bulging discs.
- Stomach muscles (rectus abdominis) are stretched during Seal.

Contraindications:

- This shape can aggravate back injuries and issues.
- Avoid pressing the belly into the floor if pregnant (use bolsters under the pelvis and forearms for support).
- If you feel any sharp pains in this shape, you must come out.
- Avoid dropping the head back if you have any neck injuries or issues.

How to get into the form:

- Begin lying on your stomach.
- Come up onto the elbows and take hold of the opposite elbow with each hand, to make sure that they are shoulder-width apart.
- Try to align your elbows under your shoulders, but if this feels too strong, then shuffle the elbows further forwards.
- Palms can be flat on the floor and toes untucked, so that the top of the feet rest flat against the floor.

Modifications:

- You can place a block or a bolster underneath the chest or armpits to give you some extra support and take the pressure off of your elbows, neck and shoulders.
- You can intensify the shape, by coming up onto your hands and then bringing the hands in closer to the hips.
- The closer the hands come to the hips, the more intense the stretch and backbend in Seal form (don't hold for too long and slide the hands forward or consider coming back down onto the elbows if sensations become too strong for you).
- You can bend the knees to intensify the stretch in either Sphinx or Seal.

- You can drop the head back to open the throat and chest, but avoid if you have neck injuries or issues.

How to come out of the form:

- Slowly and carefully lower your chest to the floor, removing blocks and bolsters if used.
- You can turn your head to one side and rest your cheek on your palms.
- If you want to, you can then left the knee of the leg that you are looking towards to decompress the back (make sure you repeat on the other side if you do this). Be cautious of this form if you are a combat veteran, as it may be triggering, reminding you of the 'prone' firing position.

Counter-forms:

- Resting on Heels Form.

13. Squat

I feel strong in Squat and very present. I feel rooted to the Earth, but also powerful, as I feel the strength in my thighs and back. I like to keep my head held high, activating the sternocleidomastoid muscle and facing the world with curiosity and confidence.

Benefits:

- Opens the hips.
- Strengthens the ankles.
- Releases the lower back.

Contraindications:

- Take care if hips are tight, as this can put pressure on the knees.
- Knee issues; avoid this form.
- Pregnant women; if in the later stages of pregnancy it could be wise to avoid this form, as it helps to prepare the body for childbirth and you may introduce labour.
- Avoid if you have diarrhoea.

How to get into the form:

- Stand with the feet hip width apart.
- Squat down and bring the arms in front of you.

- Place the hands in prayer and use the elbows to gently widen the inside of the thighs (just about the knees) or the shins (just below the knees).

Modifications:

- If your heels don't touch the floor, use folded blankets, cushions or blocks to support them.
- Knees and feet should point in the same direction you can spread the feet wider to help with this).
- Bringing the feet wider works the hips.
- Bringing the feet closer together works the ankles.

How to come out of the form:

- You can simply sit down onto your bottom.
- You can come back up to standing.

Counter-forms:

- Stretching the legs out in front of you in a sitting position and leaning back on the hands.
- You may want to point and flex the toes a few times or even fold forwards over the legs to release the knees and back.

- You could also 'Dangle' in a standing position, by straightening the legs and folding forwards, taking hold of the opposite elbow with each hand.

14. Upper Body Shapes

The two upper body shapes I tend to use the most are a simple Overhead Stretch and Reverse Prayer. I like to feel as though I am rooting down, whilst simultaneously growing tall when I stretch my arms overhead, like a mighty oak. With my arms in Reverse Prayer I am in a contemplative frame of mind, at the same time I feel as though I'm opening my heart and expanding ever outwards.

Overhead Stretch

Benefits:

- Stretches the back, shoulders and arms.
- A good counter to days spent working over a computer.
- Can be used with any Yin shape that leaves the arms free (e.g. Deer or Butterfly).

Contraindications:

- Issues with the shoulders, wrists or back; take care with this form and don't go fully to your edge. Seek advice from a medical professional before performing if you have any acute or chronic injuries at any of these sites.

How to get into the form:

- Interlace the fingers, paying attention to which index-finger is on top.
- As you raise the arms up overhead, turn the hands so that the palms face the ceiling.
- Hold for time.

Modifications:

- Back away from your edge if the stretch is too intense.
- Perhaps consider holding opposite elbows instead of interlacing fingers.

How to come out of the form:

- Release the fingers and allow the arms to drop back to your sides.

Counter-forms:

- Reverse the interlace of the fingers, so that the opposite index finger is on top this time.

Reverse Prayer

Benefits:

- Stretches the back, shoulders and arms.

- A good counter to days spent working over a computer.
- Can be used with any Yin shape that leaves the arms free (e.g. Deer or Butterfly).

Contraindications:

- Issues with the shoulders, wrists or back; take care with this form and don't go fully to your edge. Seek advice from a medical professional before performing if you have any acute or chronic injuries at any of these sites.

How to get into the form:

- From any sitting shape, bring the hands round behind the back.
- Fold the palms up to meet one another, fingertips pointing upwards and edges of the hands pressing gently into the back.
- Hold for time

Modifications:

- Back away from your edge if the stretch is too intense.
- Take Cow Face arm shape instead; bring your one hand high and bend the elbow as if reaching round to pat yourself on the back.

Bring the other hand behind your back and try to wriggle it up as close to the other hand as possible.

- If your hands don't meet in Cow Face, consider using a yoga strap or a belt held between the hands to extend your reach, if this feels comfortable for you.

How to come out of the form:

- Separate the palms and allow the arms to drop back to your sides.

Counter-forms:

- Interlace the fingers in front of you and stretch the palms away from you, hollowing the chest and pushing the shoulder blades apart.
- Change the interlace of your fingers so that the opposite index finger is on top and then repeat.

15. Yin Inversion

I find this shape to be deeply soothing. Sometimes just taking a moment to stop and flip my perspective, both physically and mentally, is a great way to destress and re-evaluate tricky situations in my day-to-day life. I like to use this form either to open or to close my practice - sometimes both.

Benefits:

- Can be a deeply relaxing/ restorative shape.
- Stretches the hamstrings and backs of the legs.
- Improves circulation.

Contraindications:

- Avoid if pregnant (especially past week 16) or seek a medical professional's advice before performing.
- Avoid if you have a heart condition/ blood pressure issues which mean that you shouldn't remain horizontal for a prolonged period or seek a medical professional's advice before performing and take particular care in coming up out of the shape to avoid dizziness and fainting.
- Be aware that remaining for long periods and triggering the Relaxation Response can have

adverse effects in some people (see earlier advice).

- Blood pressure can drop if you remain for a long period.
- If you remain for a long period, you may temporarily become hypoglycemic.
- Always check with your health care professional before practising if you are on any medications, particularly insulin, sedatives or cardiovascular medications.

How to get into the form:

- Begin lying on your back.
- Place a block, bolster, cushions or folded blankets underneath your lower back/ sacrum.
- Lift the legs straight up, soles of the feet or toes pointing straight up towards the ceiling – whatever feels most comfortable for you.

Modifications:

- If you are struggling to keep the legs up, bring the toes closer towards your head, so that the legs are over your body (roughly 80 degree angle).
- You could also perform this form with your legs up against the wall.
- You could use a yoga strap or belt around the ankles and hold with your hands to help give

the legs extra support, if this feels comfortable for you.

How to come out of the form:

- If not against the wall, simply lower the legs down, remove the props you were using and come into Shavasana.
- If against the wall, swing the legs to one side, slide away from the wall and come into Shavasana.

Counter-forms:

- None needed – this can be a nice shape to close your practice with or to use throughout the day for a few minutes of peace and restoration.

How to Practice

I said earlier that there were no real guidelines to practice, but I invite you to think about the following questions when you begin structuring your own sequences.

1. What do you want to achieve?

The first consideration to think about is what you want to achieve through your practice.

Do you want a more open body?

Do you want to calm the mind?

Do you want to relieve aches and pains?

Do you want to generally de-stress?

The truth is that a Yin Yoga practice can do all of these things and more, but it can also be structured to particularly focus in on some areas. For example, if you have tight hips, you might want to concentrate primarily on hip-opening shapes when you construct your sequence.

If you want to de-stress, you might like to choose just a few or even one single shape and remain in it for a prolonged period of time.

The possibilities of Yin are practically endless and I invite you to experiment with your own routines, bearing in mind the points that we discussed earlier about taking the body through all of its planes of motion and being mindful of shapes that might be triggering or uncomfortable for you.

Your practice will likely change daily, so it's OK if you don't become too attached to a set routine or, if using the same routine, it's good to know that you will likely feel different in the shapes each time you practice.

2. How long do you have?

Yin Yoga is best practised with a little and often approach. It's better to do fifteen minutes consistently, than three hours once every two weeks.

You can work out how much time you have, without making yourself feel rushed or impinging on other commitments, and structure your practice accordingly. Remember, though, that if you choose to use asymmetrical forms, you should leave yourself sufficient time to do both sides.

You might also like to leave extra time for Shavasana at the end of your practice and, if you don't have time for much else, you could just choose one form and make this the focus of your session.

3. Where is my body-mind complex today?

You will likely feel different on different days and respond to the practice in different ways, according to how your mind and/ or body receive the practice (remember that the two are inextricably linked as the body-mind complex).

As an example, on some days I like to listen to music, whereas, on others, I just like silence.

If you are carrying a new injury, please don't try to push your body as far as you usually would. Please try to be kind and respectful to your body, treating it gently and patiently. Some days you will be more comfortable and open than others.

4. Where is your edge?

Try to sense and listen to your edge – both in terms of your mental and physical comfort.

I invite you to find the place that, if you push beyond it, you will become unbearably uncomfortable in body or mind. It's fine to go to your edge and, at times, gently apply some pressure. This is how we grow, both physically and mentally.

However, don't ever force your body into a position that causes physical pain or emotional distress, even if you've been able to get into that shape easily on other days.

Know that strong physical sensations can be useful and, indeed, a slight discomfort is expected during your Yin Yoga practice. This is the whole point. When we acknowledge discomfort and accept it, rather than fighting against it, we come to realise that it's just another sensation. There really is nothing negative about it; that's just the connotation we ascribe to it when we run away from feeling.

Don't remain in a shape if you are experiencing intense physical pain to the point where you are likely to be injuring yourself, but do try to stay with the sensations that will arise and work out for yourself whether or not they are truly as harmful as you might initially perceive them to be.

When we take this lesson into our everyday lives, we can learn that even uncomfortable situations are not nearly as bad as we might have initially believed and so we can become less afraid – we experience Post Traumatic Growth.

If you like, you can pay attention to the emotions and thoughts that arise during a practice, as these are great indicators of how close you are to your mental and emotional edge.

For instance, if a repressed emotion arises that makes me feel, say, angry, I can choose to end my practice or I can sit with the emotion and observe it, allowing it to express itself and resolve. Through doing this, I will grow in terms of my emotional intelligence and ability to handle strong emotions when they arise in other day-to-day situations.

Similarly, on another day, if I'm feeling especially sad and a long, silent practice is making me feel worse, I might be wise to do some breathing exercises instead or even skip my Yin practice entirely and go for an energising walk in the sunshine.

TTR: Respect your edge in the same way that you do the rest of your body-mind complex and try to work in harmony with it, rather than against it.

5. The breath

I don't generally advocate breath control during a Yin Yoga practice, but I do strongly suggest listening to the breath. What the breath is doing is a very good indicator of whether or not a form is too strong for you.

If your breath becomes short and shallow, it's wise to back away from your mental or physical edge, as this is a good indicator that you're going too far. There's no shame in backing away from your edge, even if you could go further the day before.

If your breathing is slow and steady, this is a good indication that you are in a good place for your body and that the Relaxation Response has been triggered.

On some days, you might like to try 6:6 or alternate nostril breathing (described in a later chapter), perhaps whilst in Shavasana or the Yin Inversion. You can try these practices whilst in the other shapes, but you may lose the ability to listen to what your natural breath is trying to tell you if you do.

> *TTR: Just be present. Listen to your body-mind complex and pay attention to your breath. Therein lies the true practice of Yin Yoga.*

6. What sequences could I try?

Here are a few sample sequences to give you an idea of how you might link your forms together. None of them has a prescribed time limit, as this will vary according to each individual's level of experience, body type and time available for practise:

> *1. Hip Opening: Butterfly – Squat – Eye of the Needle – Shavasana*

> *2. Rejuvenating: Butterfly (reclined) – Reclining Twists – Yin inversion – Constructive Rest – Shavasana*

> *3. Heart-opening: Butterfly – Ankle Stretch – Sphinx or Seal – Deer – Shavasana or Reclined Butterfly*

4. _Taking the body through every plane of movement:_ Resting on Heels – Reclined Dragon – Sphinx/ Seal – Dragonfly – Ankle Stretch with Upper Body Yin - Reclined Twists - Shavasana

TTR: Every Yin Yoga session is a practise, which means you don't have to do it perfectly. There is no end goal – practice itself is the goal.

CHAPTER FIFTEEN

YOGA NIDRA

Yoga Nidra is a form of guided meditation that can bring deep relaxation for both the body and the mind.

Through the use of Body Sensing, Breath Awareness, Sankalpa, Rotation of Consciousness, Rotation of Opposites and Guided Visualisation practices Yoga Nidra systematically guides you through each level of your being (the Koshas).

It can be a way to prepare yourself for undertaking deeper states of meditation and is a good introduction to the practice for those who are unsure where to begin.

It might also simply be a lovely way to make some time for non-doing for twenty to forty five minutes and, in so doing, to power-down the Stress Response.

A Bit About Brainwaves

Unlike most adjunct therapies, which take place with the brain in the Waking State or Relaxation State, Yoga Nidra is unique in that it takes the practitioner past these states and into the Deep Sleep State with the mind fully conscious and awake, to a place beyond analysis, references, images and beliefs.

By accessing the Theta brainwave state we gain access to the unconscious patterns and behaviours that, without our knowledge, affect our conscious actions, thoughts and behaviours.

Consequently, it's possible, in this brainwave state, to make changes to these behaviours.

The predominant brainwave states we all experience are summarised briefly here:

- *Beta:* *15-30 Hz. In this state we are awake and in a normal state of consciousness.*

- *Alpha:* *9-14 Hz. Here you are relaxed and calm, perhaps in a state of meditation or creative visualisation.*

- *Theta:* *4-8 Hz. In this state you are in deep meditation or relaxation, problem-solving or undergoing hypnosis.*

- *Delta:* *1-3 Hz. Here you are experiencing a deep and dreamless sleep.*

> *- <u>Hypnogogic state:</u> In this state you are fluctuating between being awake and being asleep. You may experience vivid thoughts and dreams (similar to during REM sleep) even though you are still conscious. Many people claim that this is the gateway to the state of Yoga Nidra and you can expect to pass through it or move back and forth into it and out of it during your practice.*

Yoga Nidra isn't hypnotherapy (although some practitioners claim that it is, due to it sometimes inducing a 'trance-like' state) and it's not psychotherapy.

You are the agent for everything that you experience during a Yoga Nidra practice. The guiding voice that you're listening to merely advises you in the ways that you might like to direct your attention.

After you get the hang of it, you can practise Yoga Nidra (in its entirety or just various elements) without the aid of an audio guide.

Body Sensing, for example, can be a great stand-alone practice that you can do anytime and anywhere. It can also be an effective way to ground yourself when you're feeling dissociated or stressed.

TTR: If, when practising, anything that you experience is frightening, painful or intolerable to you, you must seek appropriate professional guidance from a medical/ mental health professional as soon as practicably possible.

The Practice of Yoga Nidra

This is a brief 'how to' that summarises how Yoga Nidra works (the books listed in the bibliography will give you lots of additional information if you're interested to learn more). The points below are simple guidelines for practice. I invite you to make your own adaptions:

1. Preparation: before you practise, make sure that your phone is switched off and that you have asked not to be disturbed.

Ensure that you're fully aware of your surroundings and the time of day.

Also ensure that you have all that you need to remain comfortable and motionless throughout the practice (cushions, props, blankets etc.). However, know that you can move any time if you feel that you need to.

Have a relatively empty stomach, as this makes it easier to avoid falling asleep.

2. *[Sankalpa]: the sankalpa is an intention set at the beginning of the practice, if used.*

More information below.

3. *Rotation of Awareness: this works on the Anna Maya Kosha. Yoga Nidra relaxes the mind by first relaxing the body. You use your mind to 'sense' or focus on different parts of your body and direct your attention there.*

4. *Breath Awareness: in this phase of Yoga Nidra we are working with Prana Maya Kosha. The mind and breath mirror one another.*

If you like you can try one of the breathing practices I describe in the next chapter or you can simply concentrate on observing the flow of your breath, if this feels comfortable for you.

5. *Rotation of Opposites: in this phase of Yoga Nidra we are working with Mano Maya Kosha. We permit the body to experience opposites of sensation (e.g. heavy and light) or opposites of emotion (e.g. sadness and joy).*

You can leave this part out if you like, which is often advisable if you are feeling particularly emotional when you practice, as it can be triggering.

6. _Resting as Awareness/ the Witness_: during this stage of Yoga Nidra we work with Vijnana Maya Kosha. There is a sense of detached presence.

Even though thoughts, emotions and bodily sensations may still arise we may begin to feel as though we are everywhere and nowhere all at once.

7. _Resting in Wholeness_: at this stage of Yoga Nidra you are working with Ananda Maya Kosha, resting as Being.

This can be a state of deep relaxation and restoration.

8. _[Visualisation]_: visualisation is not part of all Yoga Nidra traditions, so it's up to you whether or not you want to include it.

9. _[Repetition of Sankalpa]_: you can revisit the sankalpa before transitioning to full wakefulness, if a sankalpa has been used.

10. _Returning to Wakefulness/ Ending the Practice_: it's important to transition slowly and gently back to full wakefulness, to avoid feeling jarred or dissociated. Try to treat this phase in the same way that you would treat coming out of a long-held Yin shape; be slow and gentle with yourself.

Samskaras

Samskaras are internal impressions or 'grooves' left on the body-mind complex, which cause it to tend to act in certain ways, both helpful and unhelpful:

> *1. Helpful samskaras: an example of a helpful samskara is instinctively knowing not to put your hand into a fire. Helpful samskaras allow us to navigate day-to-day life without having to relearn, every day, basic survival instincts and behaviours.*
>
> *2. Unhelpful samskaras: unhelpful samskaras drive our tendencies toward limiting behaviours in a precognitive, reflexive manner. They can alter the courses of our lives and create outcomes (Karma) that we don't intend.*

We need helpful samskaras in our lives in order to keep us safe from danger. We really don't need unhelpful *samskaras* at all.

> *TTR: Unhelpful samskaras are like clouds, passing through the sky of our awareness. Sometimes this cloud lingers and we become overcast. We hold onto the belief, holding it as a truth and living from this place.*

If you have a negative belief about yourself or others, it is possible to let it go and allow your grey skies to clear.

You might want to try the following exercise to help you think about the *samskaras* that you are currently holding onto.

Exercise:

I invite you to think of a belief you hold about yourself. Perhaps someone once said that you were 'lazy' or 'chubby' or maybe you were told at school that you were 'sporty' or a 'high achiever'.

Whatever this belief is, write it down on a piece of paper or in your self-reflective journal.

Now examine this belief and try to answer the five questions that follow:

1. Have there been times when you have proved it to be true?

2. Have there been other times when you have proved it to be false?

3. Now ask yourself, do you want or need to verify that this belief is true or false?

4. Do you want or need to prove something to someone who has already long forgotten what they said?

5. Do you want this belief to be a lasting part of your truth?

If the answer to the last two questions is 'no' you have discovered a samskara that you are ready to let go of.

Rewriting Samskaras

In Yoga Nidra we use the power of Intention (*sankalpa*) to rewire our brain and to rewrite the *samskaras* that no longer serve us. The power of Intention comes from where we put our attention.

TTR: Where attention goes, energy flows.

If we focus our attention on the negatives in our lives, these will perpetuate.

If we focus our attention on the positives, however small, these will flourish and grow.

The following exercise is all about intention and attention. I invite you to try it for yourself and to see what you learn.

Exercise:

Focus your attention on your right hand.

> *Focus on feeling every aspect of your right hand, your thumb, your index finger, your middle finger, your ring finger, your little finger. Focus on your palm and focus on the back of your hand. Focus on your right hand with every ounce of your attention.*
>
> *How does your left hand feel?*
>
> *Did you even feel it at all before I mentioned it?*

In Yoga Nidra, we use a *sankalpa*, a positive intention that we wish to embody in our waking life, to create a new, helpful *samskara* in the subconscious. Instead of simply layering a positive belief over a negative belief, we actually create a new groove in the bliss body through which to channel our energy.

You can make your positive *samskaras* as deep as the Grand Canyon by repeatedly directly your focus towards them both during Yoga Nidra and your everyday life!

A Sample Script

The script below is one that I've used on myself and with others. It's intended to give you a representation of the possibilities of Yoga Nidra and how a practice might be structured. Feel free to pick and choose elements that you like and discard those that you don't.

You could record yourself reading the script to try it out or you could ask a trusted friend to read it to you.

All you need to practice is yourself and the audio.

You can practice lying in Shavasana (under a blanket if you are a chilly mortal like me and bearing in mind that your body temperature will drop as you relax) or any other position in which you feel comfortable. Legs up the wall can be quite nice, so can reclining Butterfly.

I've indicated which phase of the practice each section represents.

The most important elements for inducing the Relaxation Response and reducing stress are the Body-Sensing and Breathing sections.

You can practice these in isolation if you don't like the other bits or if you're short on time. I often like to add these two bits in at the end of a Yin Yoga practice, when I'm resting in Shavasana.

TTR: You are totally in charge of this practice. If you feel unsafe or uncomfortable at any point, simply stop.

In writing this script I was inspired primarily by the work of Dr Richard Miller and that of Swami Janakananda, who are my personal favourites to listen to and practise with.

I strongly recommend that you take a look at Dr Miller and his work, as he's an expert on working through PTSD and trauma with Yoga Nidra.

Both Dr Miller's and Swami Janakananda's audios and books are listed in the bibliography. I also recommend that you visit the Yoga Nidra Network's webpage, if you like the practice, as they have free Nidras available for you to listen to.

Again, the web address is in the bibliography.

Yoga Nidra Script:

Welcome to this Yoga Nidra practice for deep rest and wellbeing... Before you begin, make sure that you are aware of your surroundings... look around and make sure that you are aware of time and place... then, if you are ready, come to a position lying on your back in Shavasana... arms rest easily at your sides... legs are slightly apart, so that neither the feet nor the thighs are touching... take a moment to become aware of your surroundings... register the sights, sounds and smells that are with you in this moment... then, when you are comfortable and if it feels safe for you, allow your eyelids to close and the tension to flow from your body... you are about to begin the practice of Yoga Nidra...

[Pause]

Whatever you experience within the practice is absolutely fine... thoughts, feelings and sensations may arise or you may go to sleep... It doesn't matter if you do fall asleep, you will still benefit from the practice, but, if you can, try to stay awake and aware... say to yourself, now, in your mind "I am awake, I am aware, I am practising Yoga Nidra".... say again the affirmation "I am awake, I am aware, I am practising Yoga Nidra"... I will repeat these words at intervals throughout the practice...

[Pause]

If you are disturbed during the practice, don't worry, you will easily be able to return... simply acknowledge the distraction, then continue to follow the sound of my voice... if you are uncomfortable, take a few moments now to move the body... after you have settled, try not to move your body again during the practice, but know that you are able to if you so wish... and now, if you will, please allow my words to become your words as you enter into the state of Yoga Nidra...

END OF PREPARATION

[Pause]

Take a moment to set for yourself a sankalpa, a heartfelt intention... a resolve that you will take with you into your waking life... make it a resolve that will enhance your daily existence... a personal resolve that has meaning only for you... the sankalpa can be for yourself or for the benefit of others... if you don't have a sankalpa in mind, that is perfectly fine too, you can practice without... otherwise, set your intention now, in the present tense and feel that it is already happening...

[Pause]

END OF SANKALPA

[Pause]

Now turn your attention to your body... feel your body resting safe and secure against the floor... feel the plane of contact between the body and the floor... feel the plane of contact between your legs and the floor... feel the plane of contact between your back and the floor... feel the plane of contact between the back of your head and the floor... feel how your entire body is supported by the floor... safe... supported... secure... the entire body is supported by the floor...

[Pause]

*Now bring your attention to your right thumb...
to your right index finger... to your right
middle finger... to your right ring finger... to
your right little finger... feel your whole
hand... feel now your right arm... the wrist...
the lower arm... the elbow... the upper arm...
your right shoulder... the whole of the right
arm... your right side, the whole way down the
torso... feel the pelvis... bring the attention
now to your right leg... to the right thigh... to
the right knee... to the right calf... to the right
ankle... to your right foot... to the right big
toe... to the second toe... to the middle toe... to
the fourth toe... to the little toe... feel your
entire right side...*

[Pause]

*Turn your attention now to your left thumb... to
your left index finger... to your left middle
finger... to your left ring finger... to your left
little finger... feel your whole hand... feel now
your left arm... the wrist... the lower arm... the
elbow... the upper arm... your left shoulder...
the whole of the left arm... your left side, the
whole way down the torso... feel the pelvis...
bring the attention now to your left leg... to the
left thigh... to the left knee... to the left calf...
to the left ankle... to your left foot... to the left*

big toe... to the second toe... to the middle toe... to the fourth toe... to the little toe... feel your entire left side...

[Pause]

Feel the throat and the sensations that are there... Now focus on the mouth... the sensations inside the mouth... the tongue... the lips... the plane between the lips, where they do not touch... bring your awareness to your nose... to your right eyebrow... the orbit of your right eye... the left eyebrow... the orbit of your left eye... feel the inside of the right ear... the outside of the right ear... the inside of the left ear... the outside of the left ear... feel both ears together... feel the whole face together... feel the entire head...

Feel your entire right hand... feel your entire left hand... feel both hands together... feel your right foot... feel your left foot... feel both feet together... feel both ankles together... feel both knees together... feel the pelvis and both hips together... feel the abdomen... feel the chest... feel the right shoulder... feel the left shoulder... feel both shoulders together... feel both elbows together... feel both wrists together... feel both hands together... feel the entire body, leaving nothing out... feel everything from the crown of the head to the very tips of the toes... feel the entire body... feel the entire body...

END OF ROTATION OF AWARENESS

[Pause]

Bring your awareness now to your breath... to your body breathing... your natural breath... you don't need to change the breath, just feel the flow of energy as you inhale and exhale... you're your natural breath... feel how the breath flows round the entire body, from the crown of the head to the very tips of the toes ...

[Pause]

Now bring your awareness to your nostrils... how does it feel when you inhale?... how does it feel when you exhale?...

[Pause]

Feel the cool, sharp air as you draw in the breath... and the warm, gentle flow as you release the breath... focus now on the right nostril... as you inhale, feel, in your mind, that you are breathing only with the right nostril... and as you exhale, feel that you are breathing only with the left nostril... inhale with the left nostril... exhale with the right nostril... inhale with the whole right side of the body... exhale with the whole left side of the body... as you inhale and exhale repeat this rotation of awareness from right to left side, left to right side...

[Pause]

Inhale with the right side... 1... exhale with the left side... 1... inhale with the left side... 2... exhale with the right side... 2... inhale with the right side... 3... exhale with the left side... 3... continue this rotation of breath, counting up as high as you can... if you lose track of your breaths part way, as soon as you realise, return the count to 1... don't worry if you do lose your count and have to start again, this is part of the process...

END OF BREATH AWARENESS

[Pause]

Now allow your breath to return to its natural rhythm... "I am awake, I am aware, I am practising Yoga Nidra"...

[Pause]

Feel that the body has become very heavy... so heavy that it is sinking into the floor... feel how the body presses into the floor... the legs are heavy, like stones... the abdomen, chest and back are heavy, pulling you down deeper... the shoulders, arms and hands are sinking into the floor... your head is heavy like a lead weight... your entire body is heavy...

[Pause]

Now feel that the body has become light... so light that it floats in sensation... the body floats... your legs are like clouds, drifting on the breeze... the abdomen, chest and back are empty and free... the shoulders arms and hands are floating... the entire body is buoyant and light...

[Pause]

The body is now heavy once more... sinking... like lead... your body is sinking deeper into the floor... heavy... the body is now light... floating... like clouds drifting on the breeze... light... go back and forth in your own mind between the sensations of heaviness and lightness... feel that your body is alternately heavy and then light... then feel, if you can, both of these sensations simultaneously... this will not happen in the mind... this is a felt sensation only... the body is both heavy and light...

[Pause]

Become aware now of sensations of warmth within your body... feel heat residing within your body... experience the sensation... allow the feeling of warmth to become fully present inside your body, as though you were lying in the midday sun...

Now become aware of the opposite sensation of cold... feel coolness somewhere within your body... perhaps it is where the air touches against your skin... become aware of the feeling of cold... allow your body to experience the cold, as though walking through a snowy landscape in the middle of winter...

And notice, now, how both heat and cold can reside within your body together... feel how some parts of your body might be warm, whereas others may feel cool... allow yourself to experience both sensations together... feel both the warmth and the cold within you simultaneously...

END OF ROTATION OF CONSCIOUSNESS (SENSING OPPOSITES)

[Pause]

"I am awake, I am aware, I am practising Yoga Nidra..."

[Pause]

Feel now the emotions that are residing within you... whatever emotions are present, allow them to come into your awareness now, without judgement... it doesn't matter whether they are positive or negative... allow the body to feel the effects of the emotions that you hold... permit the body to experience the sensation that they generate within you... feel the sensations for a moment... now let those sensations go... release the sensations and, with them, allow your emotions to dissipate... allow your emotions to pass through the sky of your being, like clouds on a sunny day... let go of your emotions and feel what is still present underneath...

[Pause]

Feel yourself as presence without your emotions... feel yourself as Atma... awareness beyond thoughts, feelings and emotions... as Atma you can rest here and simply be... you can release your thoughts, feelings and emotions and simply reside here in comfort... you can rest here in the wholeness and perfection of your being... you are not your thoughts, feelings or emotions... you are Atma... whole and perfect...

END OF RESTING IN AWARENESS

[Pause]

Allow yourself to spend a few minutes here now resting as Atma ... just resting and being... nothing to think about... nothing to do... simply resting...

[Long pause of a few minutes]

END OF RESTING IN WHOLENESS

VISUALISATION WOULD GO HERE

[Pause]

Before you begin to bring awareness back to the body, if you made a sankalpa, allow it arise within you again now... in your mind, say your sankalpa to yourself now... repeat your sankalpa to yourself a few times... affirm the wish or intention that you made, so that you can take it back with you into your waking life...

END OF REPETITION OF SANKALPA

[Pause]

And now, take a deep breath in, expanding the tummy and then the chest... and let it go...

[Pause]

If you are experiencing any physical sensations, without judgement, notice them now...

[Pause]

If you are experiencing any emotional sensations, without judgement, notice them now...

[Pause]

If you are experiencing any mental sensations, without judgement, notice them now...

[Pause]

Ask yourself what you can notice about the entire body-mind... without judgement, observe any changes that you notice within your whole self...

[Pause]

Gradually, slowly and gently, become more and more aware of the body... of the hands... of the feet... of the arms... of the legs... of the torso... of the face... of the head... feel the back of the body in contact with the ground... feel the back of the head in contact with the ground... feel that you are supported and present... feel the light weight of the cover over you... realise that there is light in the world outside your closed eyes... listen to the sounds that are with you... notice the smells that are here...

[Pause]

It's time now to come back to full awareness and wakefulness... it's time to return to the waking world...

[Pause]

Sense the room around you... sense the body again... direct your attention to your hands... direct your attention to your feet and to your legs... feel the back of the head pressing against the floor... feel the back of the body pressing against the floor... when you're ready, allow the eyelids to gently open...

[Pause]

Become more and more aware of time and space... gently bring movement back into the hands and feet... feel awareness of your surroundings... notice the sights, the sounds and the smells, as you transition back to full wakefulness... notice the colours and the light... feel yourself grounded and present in this moment... returning to the waking world from the deep and restful space that is Yoga Nidra...

END OF RETURNING TO WAKEFULNESS/ ENDING THE PRACTICE

[Pause]

Come back fully into the waking world... the practice of Yoga Nidra is now over.

Again, as with Yin Yoga, a little and often approach is best, but even practising once a week could produce a noticeable effect for you.

You may find that you don't like the practice initially (I hated it), but this is when your self-reflective journal really comes into its own.

Directly after Yoga Nidra is a great time to write down your thoughts and feelings and any sensations that you might have experienced. I did this every day for four months when I was doing my Yoga Nidra teacher training and it was intense, but incredibly revealing. It was very interesting to re-read my earliest entries at the end of the course.

I was so much lighter and brighter by the end!

CHAPTER SIXTEEN

BREATHING PRACTICES

Vagus Nerve Stimulation

We can live for over fifty days without food and for around seven days without water. Without oxygen though, unless you are a well-trained deep-sea diver, you will only last around five minutes.

There's lots of exciting research going on at the moment about the link between breathing disorders and an overactive immune system. Studies have demonstrated that proper breathing (full abdominal breaths) can improve Heart Rate Variability (HRV), which in turn reduces immune system activation. Research also shows a link between the nervous system and the breath.

You probably remember we talked a lot about the nervous system at the beginning of this book.

During deep abdominal breathing, the Vagus Nerve is stimulated. This is the nerve that triggers the Relaxation Response.

Earlier I said that Body Sensing and Breathing were the most important parts of a Yoga Nidra practice and that is precisely why; we are toning the Vagus Nerve.

Without going into too much detail about the body's nervous system, the Vagus Nerve is the nerve that comes from the brain and controls the parasympathetic nervous system.

Hopefully, you remember that the parasympathetic nervous system is the one that helps us to calm down and the one that's in charge of helping us to relax.

To give you an extreme example of just how important the Vagus Nerve is, if the Vagus Nerve doesn't release acetylcholine to the diaphragm (say because you've been poisoned or the nerve has been compromised in some other way), the brain can't communicate with it and you will stop breathing.

The Vagus Nerve is an absolutely essential communication channel that runs from the brain the whole way down the torso; it's in touch with every single vital organ. It releases acetylcholine, which is responsible for learning, memory, calming and relaxing. Helpfully, acetylcholine is also an anti-inflammatory, which counteracts the inflammatory response caused by stress (particularly prolonged stress).

Also helpfully, stimulating the Vagus Nerve really is as easy as breathing in and breathing out.

All you need to do is:

> *1. Take slower breaths.*
>
> *2. Make sure you breathe from the abdomen, fully expanding the belly as well as the chest.*
>
> *3. Ensure that your exhales are longer than your inhales (if this isn't triggering for you).*

As I mentioned earlier, some people will be triggered by breathing practices, so, if you think this might be you, please feel free to ignore the exercises and advice given in this section or I invite you to try them whenever you feel safe and comfortable enough to do so.

If you do want to try stimulating your Vagus Nerve, you could start with the exercise below:

> *Exercise:*
>
> *Inhale through the nose (or mouth, but preferably the nose), bring the breath all the way down into the lower abdomen.*

Next fill up the middle section of the torso, expanding your diaphragm and your ribs.

Finally, draw the breath into the upper chest and shoulders.

If you want to, you can hold the breath for a moment, if it feels comfortable for you.

Then, when you are ready to exhale, release the chest first.

Next allow the breath to leave the diaphragm and the ribs.

Finally, empty the lower abdomen.

Again, you can pause here for a moment between breaths if it feels comfortable for you.

This inhale and exhale is one Full Yogic Breath.

You can easily improve the tone of your Vagus Nerve, because you can do it anytime and anywhere. All you have to do is breathe.

The Full Yogic Breath from the exercise above is particularly effective. It may take a bit of getting used to, because most of us only breathe shallowly with the upper chest, but it's possible to master it with a bit of practise.

Precautions: Breath Control and Anxiety

Before we start looking at ways that we can control our breathing (*pranayama* practices if you want to use the yogic term) I want to just say a few words about breathing and anxiety.

If you're an anxious person or you've suffered from trauma, Breath Control should be approached with caution. Controlling the breath can be extremely helpful, but it can also be triggering for some people. This is why I've only included a few very simple practices here.

Breath Control can also be triggering for those of you who've previously had to utilise special breathing techniques in your careers, for instance military veterans (especially snipers) who may find the exhale brings up uncomfortable sensations for them.

I advise everyone (trauma survivor or not) to approach Breath Control practices with caution and to explore them within their own comfort and tolerance levels.

This is another of the many reasons why I'm such a massive fan of using Yin Yoga to help with trauma symptoms, because no Breath Control is required. In most hatha yoga practices you are asked to use *ujjayi* (pronounced oo-jai) breath, which is a form of Breath Control. You coordinate your movements with the breath throughout the yoga session, which can be incredibly panic-inducing in some trauma survivors.

I encourage you to explore Breath Control practices in your own time and at your own pace, in an environment where you already feel safe and secure, and to stop at once if you feel any sensations of panic or fear.

The one exception to this rule of not controlling the breath is if you're actually in the middle of a panic or anxiety attack, in which case you could try the 7/11 Breath. It slows the breathing down and, by increasing the length of the exhales, triggers the Relaxation Response and relieves the panic attack.

Breath Awareness

Breath Awareness isn't really a breath control practice as such. It's more a very simple meditation.

Whenever you remember, I invite you to just take a moment to check in with yourself, by tuning into the breath.

What's going on there?

If your breathing is fast and shallow, you're probably stressed or in pain.

If the breathing is slow and regular you're likely to be relaxed or maybe even asleep.

We did this practice in an earlier chapter, so I'm not going to repeat it again here, but you can if you want to.

TTR: One full, conscious, breath in and one full, conscious, breath out is meditation.

6:6 Breath

This breath was taught to me by Ben Wolff. If you ever get the chance to study with him, I can thoroughly recommend it. I've listed Ben's website in the bibliography, so you can look him up at your leisure.

This breathing practice is ridiculously simple. All you have to do is this:

- Inhale for the count of six seconds.

- Exhale for the count of six seconds.

And that's it.

I like to retain my breath between the inhale and the exhale for a count of two-three seconds and pause between the exhale and the next inhale for the same amount of time.

I'm not especially recommending this.

It's just something that I like to do, because it feels good to me. I like the sensation of being empty and almost floating in space in that beat between the breaths.

As you become more comfortable with the practices I've described in this book, you may start doing little experiments of your own and discover things that you find really beneficial or soothing for yourself.

Alternate Nostril Breathing

This is an easy practice that you can do anywhere.

You can perform *nadi shodhana* using your fingers to physically assist, but that's probably not going to be the easiest thing to do on the Tube during the morning commute.

I prefer to follow the breath only with my mind. I find it a deeply soothing practice, helping to bring the right and left hemispheres of the brain into unison. As we discussed earlier when we looked at Ida and Pingala, our left nostril is a calming breath, our right nostril brings energy. We need both. We need both Yin and Yang in our lives to become balanced and this practice helps to unify us.

This is the Breath-Awareness practice I used in my earlier Yoga Nidra script and it's one of my favourites.

Exercise:

Closing your eyes, if you wish, breathe as if drawing in the breath from the right side of your body. When you exhale, release the breath as if only through your left side. Then reverse the process.

Breathe in through your left side, breathe out through your right side.

In through your right.

Out through your left.

If you like, you can add counting.

Inhale through your left, one.

Exhale through your right, one.

Inhale through your right, two.

Exhale through your left, two.

Every five breaths inhaling and exhaling through both your left and your right sides together.

If you like this practice and you're in a quiet space, where you feel safe and secure, you might like to try using the fingers to physically assist.

There's a Special Yoga Way of using your fingers and your thumb to do this, but I've found that pretty much any way you physically use the hands to close the nostrils works. As ever, the internet will give you plenty of assistance if you want to learn the 'proper' way of doing it, otherwise, this is what you do:

Exercise:

- Use the fingers to close the right nostril.

- Exhale gently, but fully through the left nostril.

- Inhale through the left nostril and pause briefly.

- Simultaneously close the left nostril with your hand and release the right nostril.

- Exhale gently, but fully through the right nostril.

- Keep the left nostril closed and inhale through the right nostril.

- Pause.

- Close the right nostril, whilst simultaneously releasing the left.

- Exhale all the air back out.

This is one complete round of *nadi shodhana*.

All you have to do then is just keep repeating the cycle for however long you would like to. When you finish, you can let the hands fall comfortably away and take a few rounds of Full Yogic Breath, before allowing your breathing to return to its normal pattern.

7/11 Breath

This breath was mentioned in an earlier chapter, so I won't duplicate it again here.

I will just remind you, however, that this is the go-to breath if you're feeling panicky or anxious.

I invite you to use it as often as you feel you need to.

TTR: The breath is the back-door to the mind.

CHAPTER SEVENTEEN

BRINGING YOGA INTO EVERYDAY LIFE

The Yamas and Niyamas are two of the limbs from the great seer Patanjali's 'Eight Limbs' of Yoga. This book covers all of the Eight Limbs, with the exception of Samadhi:

1. _Yama:_ *ethical disciplines (see below).*

2. _Niyama:_ *rules of conduct (see below).*

3. _Asana:_ *the physical practise of forms.*

4. _Pranayama:_ *breathing practices.*

5. _Pratyahara:_ *withdrawal of the senses (see the chapter on Yoga Nidra).*

6. _Dharana:_ *concentration (see Body Sensing in the chapter on Yoga Nidra).*

> 7. _Dhyana:_ meditation (this includes Yin Yoga practice, Yoga Nidra and Breath Awareness).
>
> 8. _Samadhi:_ absorption or bliss.

Samadhi is the ultimate goal of all yogis; the liberation of the 'soul' from the material body and the endless cycle of life and death.

However, I believe that when you've lived with trauma for a prolonged period of time, any lessening of your symptoms is in itself a form of Samadhi; a way to find your own 'Heaven on Earth'.

But back to Patanjali.

Patanjali lived ages ago and is famous for writing the Yoga Sutras, which are a collection of sayings about what yoga is and how it should be performed. Scholars don't actually agree on when he lived and when he wrote these aphorisms down (if it was in fact _him_ that wrote it all down and not a collection of people), so I won't specify dates. It was sometime before 400CE.

There are lots ancient writings about what yoga is and how to do yoga (for instance the Hatha Yoga Pradipika), but Patanjali's book is widely considered to be one of the most important and is often referred to in modern day yoga practice.

Yoga teachers especially like talking about the Yamas and Niyamas:

1. Because it makes them sounds smart.

2. Because it makes them seem Enlightened.

3. Because they are actually quite useful little guidelines for everyday life.

I'm going to give you a list of what each Yama and Niyama is and then I'm going to talk in a bit more detail about the one that is most important to me.

You might disagree with me and decide that some of the others are more significant, in which case you might choose to adopt them as your own guiding principles.

The Yamas, the 'ethical disciplines' are as follows:

1. Ahimsa: non-violence.

2. Satya: truthfulness.

3. Asteya: non-stealing.

4. Brahmacharya: moderation/ self-control.

5. Aparigraha: non-coveting/ non-attachment.

The Niyamas, the 'rules of conduct', go like this:

1. _Shaucha:_ purification/ clearness of mind, speech and body.

2. _Samtosha:_ contentment.

3. _Tapas:_ discipline.

4. _Svadhyaya:_ self-study/ self-reflection.

5. _Ishvara Pranidhana:_ devotion.

The Yamas may be thought of as the 'don'ts' and the Niyamas can be thought of as the 'dos'. I fail pretty miserably at most of the Niyamas, but I like to think I'm pretty good at the Yamas.

Of the five Yamas, Aparigraha is the most important to me, so I will expand on it a little more.

Aparigraha

Aparigraha is the practice of non-attachment, non-possessiveness or non-greediness.

Or, as a character from a well-known children's film would say; let it go!

This is a lesson that I need to remind myself of frequently. In our culture we are results-driven, always told to strive to be the best, defined by our jobs and our possessions. Even if we choose to step away from those traps, we're still attached to other things we care about; family, friends, ambitions, dreams, hopes… the list goes on _ad infinitum_.

But what happens if we stop being attached to all of those things?

A while ago, I submitted a manuscript (not this one) to a publisher and waited five agonising weeks for a response. During that time, because I was so attached to the idea of having the manuscript published, I pretty much tortured myself daily about the outcome.

I should've known that investing so much energy in a decision that was out of my hands was entirely fruitless and only served to cause me needless suffering.

And that is the point of Aparigraha.

It's not an attitude of non-caring, but a way to separate yourself from outcome.

Things will happen, whether you worry about them or not.

Family and friends will be fine (or won't be) whether or not you attach yourself to their problems.

You will be promoted at work (or you won't be) regardless of whether you are lying awake at night rehashing yesterday's meeting and over-analysing every single word that was said.

Aparigraha means that what will be, will be, but you can free yourself from suffering by choosing not to be attached to the outcome either way.

And Aparigraha, ultimately, is freedom.

Trauma survivors need to take back agency. We need to be free from the control of others, from the minor stresses and the pressures of everyday life. We can do this most effectively by taking up residence through Aparigraha.

If you're not attached to outcome, then the 'thing' (whatever it is) has no power over you.

If you don't attach to the negative thoughts, feelings and emotions that resurface as a result of surviving your trauma, then they have no power to hurt you.

Non-attachment is not dissociation.

Non-attachment is *accepting*.

Aparigraha means knowing that things are as they are and that you are here and now.

The past is the past.

You can choose to accept it and to let it go.

Using the Yamas and Niyamas

If you want to, I invite you to explore your own attitudes towards the Yamas and Niyamas, using the exercise below:

Exercise:

If you like, look again at the list of Yamas and Niyamas at the beginning of this chapter.

Take out your self-reflective journal or some blank paper and write down a few that you feel drawn towards.

Perhaps you are already practising some of these principles in your life or maybe you would like to start practicing some.

For each Yama/ Niyama that you have chosen write a brief description of what this guideline means to you.

If you want, you could put the list somewhere visible (like stick it to the front of the fridge or the wall near your bed) and refer back to it each day.

I bet that, before you know it, you'll have begun to make the Yamas and Niyamas that you have chosen a part of your everyday life and you'll soon find that even more of them creep in, as your attitudes start shifting and you begin to see the world in a different way.

I hope that this chapter helped you to understand that the Yamas and Niyamas are not strict commandments and that each individual will apply them differently according to his or her own world view and life situation.

The Yamas and Niyamas can be useful tools for gently guiding us towards Post Traumatic Growth, allowing us to really think about what is important to us in this life and helping us to develop some level of spiritual understanding that might go beyond what we perceive in our day-to-day lives.

> *TTR: If you work towards following some or all of the Yamas and Niyamas, you will find that they tend to beget one another.*
>
> *For instance, Aparigraha and Ahimsa tend to lead to less self-blame, which in turn leads to greater contentment (the Niyama Samtosha).*
>
> *Yoga really is a clever system that works without you even realising it!*

CHAPTER EIGHTEEN

STUFF THAT I'VE LEARNED

This final chapter really is just a list of Stuff That I've Learned that you might also find helpful. You might not, but hopefully (within the context of everything that we've already covered in this book) at least some of it will make sense.

I've also included the full Loving-Kindness meditation that you may have tried at the beginning of this book and I invite you to practise it whenever you feel ready to.

So, here we go, my list of STILs:

1. Self Love.

It's not selfish to prioritise yourself – no one else will – and if you are not OK, everyone and everything you interact with won't be OK either, because you will respond to people and situations from a place of not-OK-ness.

Before the world finds peace, everyone must first find peace within themselves.

Loving yourself is the key to loving everyone and everything else. And when I say 'love', what I really mean here is 'accept'. Acceptance allows us to practice Aparigraha and to live a life of freedom.

2. Remember That Everyone Is Just Doing The Best They Can.

This is an important STIL when deciding how to react and how to apply some of the other STILs below.

Before you condemn yourself for your previous behaviour or some of the ways that you might behave now, remember that you were and still are just doing the best you can.

Similarly, even when people annoy you or seem to be getting it wrong, you have to remember that they too are only doing the best they can.

So, stop. Think. React accordingly (and with a little Ahimsa thrown in for good measure).

3. Pay Attention.

How are you feeling today?

How do certain people, places and situations make you feel?

When you start really listening to your body, paying attention to what it's trying to tell you, rather than fighting with it all the time, you should be able to determine what makes you feel better and what makes you feel worse.

Focus on the positives and avoid the negatives where possible.

Remember, whatever we focus on expands, so make sure that you become an expert at understanding what your body needs from you to feel safe, nurtured and loved.

After all, it's the only home you have to live in.

4. Remove Toxic People.

This is an easy one and all about Self Love.

If people make you feel unsafe or upset or if they trigger you in any way, then remove them politely, but firmly from your life. Give them a chance to modify their behaviour, by explaining how it negatively impacts upon your mental and physical health and, if they choose not to change the way they act, you can then decide to part ways.

You don't need them or the turmoil that they bring in your life.

Protect yourself first and always.

5. Have A Hate Hump.

An ex-boyfriend taught me this (not because he's in mine, but because he had one).

I know that this is a book about yoga and yogis are supposed to be all peace and love, but you are human.

Some things will piss you off.

You have the choice to either let these things annoy you or you can put them in your hate hump and forget about them.

Just every now and again be sure to go in and give your hump a quick spring clean. You don't want your hump to get too heavy, so make sure you're not putting petty annoyances in there. Like, for instance, if the neighbour's cat is in there, it probably shouldn't be, unless it's a creature from hell that tries to tear your face off every time you walk out of the front door.

Save Hate Hump space for the Really Big Things (usually the stuff that goes against your basic moral principles).

After all, no one wants to end up looking like a Hate Camel.

6. Cat Bellies And Pony Noses.

These are just two of my favourite things.

It's good to have favourite things, no matter how bizarre.

I like to kiss my pony on the nose when I feed her apples, because it smells nice and cuddly.

I like to kiss my cat on the belly when I cuddle her, because it smalls all cosy and furry.

Apparently I'm not the only weirdo on the planet, because my pony and cat owning friend also does and likes exactly the same thing.

Try it. You never know, you just might like it too.

7. Two Bananas And A (Non-alcoholic) Beer.

It's OK to sometimes indulge in junk, such as when I think two bananas and a beer is an adequate dinner or when it seems appropriate to eat an entire tub of vegan ice-cream in the evening, even though I only had nuts for breakfast and chips for lunch.

I no longer beat myself up about my occasional terrible food/ lifestyle choices.

Some days I eat well, other times I don't.

This STIL can be applied to life in general. You don't always have to do The Right Thing. Sometimes it's perfectly fine to just do what feels good to you at the time.

8. Do Things That Scare You.

I don't mean this in the way of things that trigger and terrify you and turn you into a gibbering mess. I mean do things that challenge you, that take you out of your comfort zone, but only when you feel ready to.

We traumatised folks are very good at constructing a comfort zone that is essentially comprised of our bedroom and maybe the bathroom and the kitchen.

This is not enough.

This is not living.

It may be OK on days when we are feeling triggered and really unsafe, but we need to be brave and push our limits.

Remember our chapter on Post Traumatic Growth.

We grow in the spaces that challenge us, the point at which we meet our edge.

Like when I did my Yin training and on the last day moved my mat away from the wall, so that I had other people all around me. It was scary as hell and it took me days to get there, but I did it.

A little bit of fear and discomfort is good for you.

A lot is bad.

Apply STILs 1 and 16 here.

9. It's OK To Cry.

Whether you're male or female crying is fine.

It's just your body's way of discharging pent-up energy.

Remember when we talked about the body-mind complex and how emotions cause physical reactions within the body?

That's all crying is.

If you don't let the tears come out, all you do is add another pile of grime to your energetic sludgeberg and no-one needs that.

So sob your heart out and feel better for it.

The only exception to this STIL is if you're crying all the time, then something a little more complicated is going on and it's probably time to visit your GP or mental health professional for a bit of guidance.

10. You Can't Do All The Things.

Believe me, I know, I've tried.

Trauma makes us very good at throwing ourselves into anything and everything, so that we don't have to deal with that horrible energetic backlog.

All that this ultimately achieves is burnout.

Your body will give up on you at some point, because it's just a machine and, when it does, you'll have to face the things that you've been running from.

And then, all Hell breaks loose and you end up like I did for a while, lying on the sofa each day, drugged up to the eyeballs on Fluoxetine, watching every single episode of Supernatural and wondering how on Earth you ended up there.

In conclusion, you can't do All The Things, so please don't try to.

11. Everybody Is Somebody Else's Weirdo.

Just be you.

It doesn't matter if you like strange things like cat bellies and pony noses.

It doesn't matter if you spend most of your days in yoga pants and enjoy doing the 'No Pants Victory Dance' when you beat your significant other at Nine Card Brag.

All of your peculiar little quirks are what make you, well, you.

You are wonderful and perfect just as you are, so don't try to change.

Not for anyone.

Always remember STIL 1 and love yourself, as you are today, as you were yesterday and as you will be tomorrow.

12. Stand For Something Or Fall For Anything.

This is kind of a tricky one and will bring you into opposition with others, as well as activating STIL 11.

You can't agree with everyone about everything all of the time, so there's no point in pretending to.

Decide what things you really care about and then stick by them.

Don't be afraid to learn and to change your mind about things if new information or experience presents itself, but make sure that you stand up for the things that you really believe in.

It could be as simple as becoming vegetarian when your entire family enjoys a whole roast pig every Sunday. If you truly believe that you shouldn't eat the little porker, then stick to your guns.

By standing up for things that you believe in, you are practising STIL 1. You are showing self-love and letting yourself know that it's perfectly OK to be exactly who you are.

13. Forgiveness.

It doesn't have to be divine.

It's important to learn to forgive both yourself and others.

This helps to ensure that your Hate Hump doesn't get too full (STIL 5) and also ensures you don't end cutting too many people out of your life or falling out with your entire family (STILs 3 and 4).

It also helps you to activate STIL 1 and ensures that you are practising self-love by forgiving yourself for your mistakes.

Forgiving is just another word of accepting, which we already know is Aparigraha – freedom.

14. Learn From Your Mistakes.

We all make mistakes, because none of us are perfect.

Mistakes are fine, as long as you learn from them. For instance, to paraphrase Einstein, who we all know was a smart guy: don't keep doing the same thing the same way and expecting a different result.

Do things wrong, sure, but forgive yourself. Then learn from that misjudgment and move on.

15. It's OK To Fail.

I do it a lot.

I am a failure.

And I'm fine with it.

It took me about a million attempts to pass my driving test and four goes to find a military service that would have me.

But, you know what?

I kept going.

I kept failing, but I kept trying.

It's OK to fail.

What it's not OK to do is not to try.

You only succeed by failing, so make sure that you are the biggest failure going!

16. Moderation.

One of our Yamas; Brahmacharya.

Don't overdo stuff, whether it's food or work or socialising.

Too much of anything can be bad for you.

Too much chocolate? Weight gain and potentially diabetes.

Too much exercise? Shin splints and over-use injuries.

Too much forgiveness? People walk all over you and treat you badly, because you didn't draw a line beyond which their bad behaviour couldn't be forgiven.

Moderation is the key. It's a form of self-love; a way to protect yourself from yourself and from others.

Life is a balance of Yin and Yang that we can achieve by practising moderation.

17. Know Thyself.

This is a well-known Ancient Greek adage.

It's pretty much a summation of self-love and getting rid of toxic people and moderation and forgiveness. It's about understanding you and what makes you tick.

I often tell myself that I'll give up chips, because I eat too many of them and one day I'm going to get incredibly fat and develop a chronic health condition. However, in reality, I never do.

I like chips.

They make me happy.

So now I apply STIL 16 and try to eat them in moderation.

I can do this competently and without judgement or self-punishment, because I know myself.

18. Find Your Power.

This STIL is about learning to say 'yes' to things, but also learning to say 'no'.

When you find your power you feel happy and confident to stand your ground and make choices that are best for you. It's an extension of STIL 17, knowing yourself, and STIL 1, self-love.

Finding your power isn't about being a bitch or a bully, it's simply about being able to say; "This is me, this is what I like and this is what I don't like, so I'm going to do this and not do that."

Finding your power isn't about judging others or bullying others into your way of thinking. It's about making choices that are right for you and that nourish you and the life that you have chosen to live.

Finding your power isn't about right or wrong.

It's about choice.

19. No-one Ever Died From Being Offended.

An opinion is just an opinion.

No matter how many people will try to convince you otherwise, an opinion that causes offence is not cause for outrage. An opinion isn't fact and an opinion may be expressed from a good place or a bad place.

Either way, if I offend you, that's just tough luck, because that's my opinion and your offence doesn't take priority over my opinion.

You can choose to be offended.

Just as I can choose to have an opinion (be it 'right' or 'wrong').

They are both just choices.

You won't die from your offence any more than I will thrive off of my opinion.

There are a couple of caveats here; firstly, if someone is bigger than you and likely to punch your lights out if you offend them, it's probably better to follow STIL 1 and keep your mouth shut.

Secondly, if you really value that person and know that voicing your opinion might hurt them and damage your relationship with them irrevocably you might want to think again about how important it is for you to make your point of view known.

20. Love – Let It In.

This is the STIL that makes me most uncomfortable in that very British way.

I'm not all about the hugging and the touchy-feeling, especially when it's with people I don't know that well. I still find it hard to trust, which is a fairly normal response in trauma survivors, but I'm learning.

Love doesn't take anything from us, it only makes us stronger.

Yes, you can get hurt if you love someone, but only if you choose to be hurt.

If you give love unconditionally and don't receive anything back, what's lost?

If you give your love unconditionally and receive love back, what's gained?

Plenty.

In my opinion, it's worth the risk of putting yourself out there.

Creating Your Own STILs

You've read through all of mine. You can borrow some of them if you like to or you can think of some of your own. There's a little space for you to do that here or maybe you want to use your self-reflective journal.

As ever, the choice is yours!

If you want to, I invite you to add your own STILs here:

> *Exercise:*
>
> *1.*
>
> *2*
>
> *3.*
>
> *4.*
>
> *5.*
>
> *6.*
>
> *7.*
>
> *8.*
>
> *9.*
>
> *10.*

Loving-Kindness Full Meditation

And so, we come now to the final exercise.

Yoga and, through it, the process of healing, isn't about getting into fancy shapes or only eating kale, it's really about becoming more compassionate towards both yourself and others.

You should always take priority, but that doesn't mean that you can't also extend some of that love, that 'acceptance' towards the rest of the world.

The theory goes that accepting others, even those we've previously had cause to dislike or to hate, is a way of being kind to ourselves, because it increases our positive emotions and reduces the negative ones.

Remember the Hate Hump. You don't want to be carrying around so much anger and dislike that it starts to weigh you down. If you do, you aren't being kind to yourself and you'll just end up making yourself feel worse.

If you'd like to give the full Loving-Kindness meditation a try, you'll find it below:

Exercise

1. If you like, begin in a seated (or other) position that is comfortable for you.

2. You might want to give yourself a few moments during which time you allow the body to settle, before bringing your attention to your hands.

3. If it feels comfortable for you, bring the palms together in a prayer position or any other position that you prefer. I invite you to notice any sensations that are present in the fingers and the palms and the backs of the hands.

4. As you breathe in and out, noticing any sensations (or lack of sensations if there aren't any) I invite you to choose a positive statement of affirmation to say aloud or think to yourself:

You could use one of these if you don't yet have any of your own:

- May I be free from inner and outer harm and danger.

- May I be safe and protected.

- May I be happy.

- May I be joyful and at ease.

To begin with, this may well be a big enough step for you to take, and you can simply end the meditation here, after repeating your positive affirmation to yourself a few times.

5. Now, if you like, think of a person (or an animal) who most invites feelings of pure, unconditional loving-kindness. Repeat your chosen phrase for this person.

6. Next, you can think of a neutral person, someone whom you neither strongly like nor strongly dislike. Repeat your phrase again for this person and see if you can welcome in a feeling of tenderness or care for their welfare.

7. You could rest here for a few moments, simply noticing the sensations within your hands and within the rest of your body (if there are any) or paying attention to the breath if this feels comfortable to you, before moving to the next step.

8. You can take a moment here to allow the feelings of loving-kindness and your accompanying phrase to spread throughout your whole body-mind complex and noticing any sensations that arise.

9. Next you could send your feelings of loving-kindness out towards your immediate surroundings, including every living being in this circle.

You could use phrases such as:

- May all beings be safe and happy.

- May all beings live joyously.

- May all beings in existence live in safety, happiness and health.

10. Finally, I invite you to try radiating loving-kindness out towards all living beings, perhaps imagining the Earth spinning within the vastness of the universe.

You may want to use a phrase such as:

- May all living beings everywhere be happy, be peaceful and be free from suffering.

You can stay with your feelings of living-kindness as long as you like, perhaps just noticing any sensations that arise within the body-mind complex.

I invite you to practice this meditation as often as you feel able and, if you like, to note down in your self-reflective journal how you feel before and after. It might also be interesting for you to see if your feelings have changed after a few weeks or months of practising.

And that's all the wisdom I have for you right now.

Thank you for reading my little book. I hope it helps you on your journey of healing, even if just a little bit.

May you be happy, may you be healthy, may you be safe, may you be free from suffering and may you live joyously!

May you always be exactly where you're supposed to be.

Namaste.

BIBLIOGRAPHY

Books

Brightening our Inner Skies, Yin and Yoga, Norman Blair, MicMac Margins, 2016

Insight Yoga, Sarah Powers, Shambala, 2008

YinSights, A Journey into the Philosophy and Practice of Yin Yoga, Bernie Clark, 2017

The Complete Guide to Yin Yoga, The Philosophy and Practice of Yin Yoga, Bernie Clark, White Cloud Press, 2011

The Yin Yoga Kit, The Practice of Quiet Power, Biff Mithoeffer, Healing Arts Press, 2006

The Modern Yoga Bible, Christina Brown Godsfield, 2017

Trauma and Recovery, The Aftermath of Violence – From Domestic Abuse to Political Terror, Judith Herman, Basic Books, 1997

The Body Keeps the Score, Mind, Brain and Body in the Transformation of Trauma, B. van der Kolk, Penguin Books, 2015

Trauma-Sensitive Yoga in Therapy, Bringing the Body into Treatment, David Emerson, W. W. Norton and Company, 2015

Overcoming Trauma through Yoga, Reclaiming Your Body, D. Emerson and E. Hopper, North Atlantic Books, 2011

The iRest Program for Healing PTSD, A Proven-Effective Approach to Using Yoga Nidra Meditation and Deep Relaxation Techniques to Overcome Trauma, R. Miller, Raincoast Books, 2015

The Relaxation Response, H. Benson, Wing Books 1975

Brightening Our Inner Skies Yin and Yoga, N. Blair, MicMac Margins, 2016

The Complete Guide to Yin Yoga, The Philosophy and Practice of Yin Yoga, B. Clark, White Cloud Press, 2012

Asana, Pranayama, Mudra, Bandha, Swami Satyananda Saraswati, Bihar School of Yoga, (reprint) 2008

Yoga Nidra, Swami Satyananda Sarawati, Yoga Publications Trust, 1974 **[N.B. Following accusations of child abuse at some of Satyananda's Ashrams this book is now widely removed from reading lists and rightly so. However, it remains one of the original and most informative texts on Yoga Nidra, so is included here to be read at your discretion.]**

Yoga Nidra, The Art of Transformational Sleep, K. Desai, Lotus Press, 2017

Yoga Nidra for Complete Relaxation and Stress Relief, J. Lusk, Raincoast Books, 2015

Yoga Nidra, A Meditative Practice for Deep Relaxation and Healing, R. Miller, Sounds True, 2005, 2010

CDs

Experience Yoga Nidra Guided Deep Relaxation, Swami Janakananda, Bindu Publishers, remastered 2012 [**N.B. the longer practice is definitely not suitable for those suffering from symptoms of trauma and the pairs of opposites (emotions, dark and light, freezing cold, extreme heat can be disturbing for many without trauma).**]

Yoga Nidra Meditation Extreme Relaxation of Conscious Deep Sleep, Swami Jnaneshvara Bharati, Tranquility Productions, 2003

Yoga Nidra, A Meditative Practice for Deep Relaxation and Healing, R. Miller, Sounds True, 2005, 2010

iRest Meditation, Restorative Practices for Health, Resiliency and Well-Being, R. Miller, Sounds True, 2015

Websites

http://www.yogawithnorman.co.uk/Bernie Clark

http://www.yinyoga.com/bernie_clark.php

http://paulgrilley.com/Sarah Powers

http://www.biffmithoeferyoga.com/The Yoga Clinic

http://www.yoganidranetwork.org/users/ben-wolff

https://www.theyogaclinic.co.uk/

https://sarahpowers.com/sp/

http://www.yoganidranetwork.org/downloads

https://www.yogacampus.com/

http://www.traumasensitiveyoga.com/

ABOUT THE AUTHOR

Sara Waymont is a therapeutic artist and yoga teacher. She formerly served with the RAF Reserves and is an ISAF Accredited War Artist. This book was developed to support Sara's work with veterans on the Veterans For Wildlife 'Footprints of Hope' programme.

Sara is trained in Hatha Yoga, Yin Yoga, Yoga Nidra and TRiM.

43677734R00139

Made in the USA
Middletown, DE
27 April 2019